Speak Japanese Today!

A Little Language Goes a Long Way!

Boyé Lafayette De Mente

Phoenix Books / Publishers

ISBN: 0-914778-46-3

About the Author

Boyé Lafayette De Mente has been involved with Japan since the late 1940s as a member of a U.S. intelligence agency, student, journalist, and editor. He is the author of more than 50 books on Japan, Korea and China, including the first ever on the Japanese way of doing business: *Japanese Etiquette & Ethics in Business (1959), and How to Do Business with the Japanese (1962).* His other books on Japan include:

KATA—The Key to Understanding & Dealing
With the Japanese
Japan's Cultural Code Words—233 Key Terms that Explain
the Attitudes and Behavior of the Japanese
NTC's Dictionary of Japan's Business Code Words
Japanese Etiquette—Know the Rules that Make the Difference
Business Guide to Japan—A Quick Guide to Opening Doors
and Closing Deals
Asian Face Reading—Unlock the Secrets Hidden
in the Human Face
Japan Unmasked—The Character & Culture of the Japanese
The Japanese Samurai Code—Classic Strategies for Success
Samurai Strategies—42 Martial Arts Secrets from
Musashi's Book of Five Rings
Samurai Principles & Practices that Will Help Preteens & Teens
in School, Sports, Social Activities & Choosing Careers
Sex and the Japanese—The Sensual Side of Japan
Japan Made Easy—All You Need to Know to Enjoy Japan
Dining in Japan—The Etiquette, the Language and the Choices
Shopping in Japan—Getting the Most out of Your ¥en
The Secrets of Japanese Design

CONTENTS

PART 10

Home-Visit Hosting

PART 11

Accidents & Illnesses

PART 12

Emergency Situations

PART 13

Measurements

PREFACE

A Little Language Goes A Long Way!

This book is designed for quick-and-easy use by people who want—or need—to communicate in Japanese about basic day-to-day topics.

With just a little practice you can communicate as many as five hundred key concepts with only a 100-word vocabulary. *Speak Japanese Today* contains more than 700 key words— which is close to the total number of words most people use in their own language during the course of a day.

The key to using the book effectively is in pronouncing the Japanese words correctly—a much easier task than most might think.

How to Pronounce Japanese

Japanese words are made up of syllables that have exact pronunciations, with far fewer variations than one finds in English and many other languages.

Like Hawaiian, the Japanese language has only a few sounds. The entire Japanese "syllabic alphabet" is based on only six sounds: ah, ee, uu, eh, oh and n (pronounced as the n in bond).

All you have to do to master Japanese pronunciation is learn these sounds and their simple derivatives.

Here are all of the syllables making up the Japanese language, along with phonetic equivalents. Just pronounce the phonetics in standard English, and the sounds will come out "in Japanese."

Chart #1

A	I	U	E	O
ah	ee	uu	eh	oh
KA	KI	KU	KE	KO
kah	kee	kuu	kay	koe
SA	SHI	SU	SE	SO
sah	she	sue	say	so

TA	CHI	TSU	TE	TO
tah	chee	t'sue	tay	toe

NA	NI	NU	NE	NO
nah	nee	nuu	nay	no

HA	HI	HU	HE	HO
hah	he	who	hay	hoe

MA	MI	MU	ME	MO
mah	me	muu	my	moe

YA		YU		YO
yah		yuu		yoe

RA*	RI	RU	RE	RO
rah	ree	rue	ray	roe

N
nnh (as the n in the word bond)

GA	GI	GU	GE	GO
gah	ghee	guu	gay	go

ZA	ZI	ZU	ZE	ZO
zah	jee	zoo	zay	zoe

DA	JI	ZU	DE	DO
dah	jee	zoo	day	doe

BA	BI	BU	BE	BO
bah	bee	buu	bay	boe

PA	PI	PU	PE	PO
pah	pee	puu	pay	poe

* The "R" sound in Japanese is close to the "L" sound in English, requiring a slight trilling or rolling to get it right. The D and Z sounds are virtually the same in the case of ZI and JI.

Chart #2

The following syllables are combinations of some of those appearing above. Two primary syllables are combined into one simply by merging the pronunciation.

RYA	RYU	RYO
r'yah	r'yuu	r'yoe
(Roll the R's a bit.)		

MYA	MYU	MYO
m'yah	m'yuu	m'yoe

NYA	NYU	NYO
n'yah	n'yuu	n'yoe

HYA	HYU	HYO
h'yah	h'yuu	h'yoe

CHA	CHU	CHO
chah	chuu	choe

SHA	SHU	SHO
shah	shuu	show

KYA	KYU	KYO
k'yah	que	q'yoe

PYA	PYU	PYO
p'yah	p'yuu	p'yoe

BYA	BYU	BYO
b'yah	b'yuu	b'yoe

JA	JU	JO
jah	juu	joe

GYA	GYU	GYO
g'yah	g'yuu	g'yoe

When pronouncing the syllables in the second chart, keep in mind that they are to be pronounced as "one" syllable, not two. Byu (b'yuu), for example, should be run together; not pronounced as (bee-you), but as the "Beu" in "Beulah."

Practice on these pronunciation charts until you can say each syllable easily and smoothly, without having to think about it. Before long you will be able to recognize individual syllables in the Japanese words you see and hear. The word *arigato* (thank you), for example, is made up of four syllables: a-ri-ga-to (ah-ree-gah-toe).

Don't forget to trill the r syllables a bit, as if they were Spanish. In fact, most of the single (uncombined) syllables in Japanese are pronounced almost exactly the same as Spanish. The A's are pronounced as ah's, the I's as ee's, and so on.

In Japanese the H and G letters are always pronounced hard, as in HO and GO. The consonants b, d, j, k, m, n, p, t and y are pronounced exactly as they are in English. Ch is pronounced as the ch in cherry.

Double consonants are common in Japanese, and it is important to distinguish between single and double consonants in words because the meanings are different. I have accounted for the differences in pronunciation of double consonants by the use of phonetics. The popular word *kekko* (meaning wonderful), for example, is pronounced as keck-koh.

The vowels i and u are often silent in Japanese words—a custom that developed over time simply because it makes the words easier to pronounce. The past tense of "to be," deshita, is pronounced desh-tah, instead of day-she-tah).

There are no true L or V sounds in Japanese, and they do not appear in the list of syllables. When the Japanese attempt to pronounce these letters in English words the L often comes out as an R and V as a B.

The vowels in many Japanese words are accented, while others are long (stressed). In the Romanized spelling of Japanese the accent and stress marks in printed materials can be, and generally are, indicted by an accent mark above the vowel or a line over the vowel if it is to be stressed.

Again, these differences can be critical. A *kiji* (kee-jee), for example is a newspaper article. A *kiji* (kee-jeee) is a pheasant. Whenever possible, I have attempted to account for accents and stresses in their phonetic pronunciation.

Again, the secret to using this book to communicate in Japanese is to pronounce the English phonetics for each word as standard English, practicing each sentence enough times that it comes out in a smooth flow.

The Japanese Language Is Not so Mysterious!

In earlier times Westerners regarded the Japanese language as mysterious and virtually impossible to learn. But this reaction was based on the complicated Chinese ideograms traditionally used to write the language and the fact that until modern times

Japanese language learning materials were practically non-existent.

Japanese is, in fact, much less difficult to learn than many of the world's other languages, and its mysteriousness quickly disappears once you get behind the facade presented by the Chinese characters and the auxiliary phonetic writing systems that are used in conjunction with the ideograms.

The reading problem associated with foreigners learning conversational Japanese was solved in the 1860s by an American medical missionary to Japan, James Curtis Hepburn, who created a system of spelling the sounds of the language with the same Roman letters that are used to write English. After that, anyone wanting to learn how to speak Japanese did not have to first learn how to read the complicated Chinese pictograms, although they too lose their forbidding image once you begin studying them.

Japanese written in Roman letters is referred to as *Roma ji* (Roe-mah jee), which literally means "Roman letters." The Chinese ideograms are called *Kan ji* (Kahn jee), which means "Chinese letters."

The grammatical structure of Japanese differs from English [instead of being subject-verb-object, it is subject-object-verb], but once you stop mentally comparing it with English [and thinking of it as being "backwards"], this "problem" also disappears. For example:

Watakushi no namae wa De Mente desu
(Wah-tahk-she no nah-my wah De Mente dess)

Grammatically this is: My name De Mente is. But the meaning is exactly the same as: My name is De Mente. Another example:

Anata no namae wan nan desu ka?
(Ah-nah-tah no nah-my wah nahn dess kah?)
Your name what is?

In other words: What is your name?

Another key point in Japanese is the lack of definite and indefinite articles (a, an, the), and the virtual lack of the plural form. *Hon* (hoan) means book or books, depending on the usage. You can't add an "s" or anything else to it and get "books." Example:

Kore wa anata no hon desu ka?

(Koh-ray wah ah-nah-tah no hoan dess kah?)
Is this your book?
Are these your books?

There are variations in personal pronouns but they are easy to master.

I
Watakushi (wah-tahk-she) used by both males and females.
Watashi (wah-tah-she) used by females.

We
Watakushi-tachi (wah-tahk-she-tah-chee)
Watashi-tachi (wah-tah-she-tah-chee) / female

You (singular)
Anáta (ah-naah-tah)

You (plural)
Anáta-tachi (ah-naah-tah-tah-chee)

He
Anókatá (ah-noh-kah-taah) / polite
Anóhitó (an-noh-ssh-tohh) / common

She
Anókatá (ah-noh-kah-taah) or kánojo (kaah-no-joe)

They
Anóhitótachi (ah-noh-ssh-toh-tah-chee) / common
Anókatágata (ah-noh-kah-taah-gah-tah) / polite

There are three types of adjectives in Japanese. One that ends in an "i" preceded by another vowel, another type that is formed by adding "na" to certain nouns, and a third type that is formed by adding the particle "no" after certain nouns. Examples:

Takai yama (tah-kigh yah-mah)
High mountain

Omoshiroi na hanashi (oh-moh-she-roy nah hah-nah-she)
Interesting talk, conversation

Nihon no hitó (Nee-hoan no ssh-toh)
Japanese person

There are, of course, similar rules for creating adverbs, but rather than trying to remember these rules it is far better to learn how to create them the same way children learn languages—by learning them in phrases and sentences.

Superlatives are easy to handle in Japanese. You just put *ichibán* (ee-chee-bahn) or *móttomo* (moat-toh-moh) in the front of words. Examples:

Ichibán ii restaurant (ee-chee-bahn ee restaurant)
The best restaurant

Ichibán yasui kippu (ee-chee-bahn yah-sooey keep-poo)
The cheapest ticket

Ichibán by itself means first or number one. *Móttomo* has more of the meaning of "more," as in móttomo nagái (moat-toh-moh nah-guy), meaning "longer."

As you can see, Japanese is a syllabic language, meaning its sounds are made up of precise syllables, which greatly simplifies the pronunciation as well as the Romanized spelling of individual words.

There is, of course, an order and a rhythm to Japanese and it can be fun to study and to use. Because it is an old language and is deeply impregnated with cultural nuances, however, the Japanese are very sensitive about how it is used. It is, therefore, important that students of Japanese also learn quite a bit of the etiquette of the language.

Another key factor in the Japanese language is the presence of several thousand "loan words"—words from other languages, primarily English, that have been integrated into the daily vocabulary of the Japanese. This simplifies the learning and use of Japanese to some extent but not nearly to the degree that one might presume.

The reason for this qualification is that foreign words that are incorporated into the Japanese language are Japanized— meaning that they are restructured into Japanese syllables and thereafter pronounced in Japanese. In other words, baseball becomes *besuboru* (bay-sue-boh-rue); computer becomes *kompyuta* (kome-pyu-tah); butter becomes *bata* (bah-tah), bread becomes *buredo* (buu-ray-doe) and so on.

However, with a little practice it is possible to become quite skilled at pronouncing English words "in Japanese," thereby greatly increasing your useable "Japanese" vocabulary. (For example, most Japanese would not understand the word "building" when it is pronounced in English. But if you break it up into Japanese syllables, *birudingu* (bee-rue-deen-guu), almost everyone will understand it.

Greetings & Farewells

Obviously, the first Japanese that one should learn is how to greet, welcome and interact with people on a basic level.

Welcome!
Irasshaimase
(Ee-rah-shy-mah-say!)

Good morning
Ohaiyo gozaimasu
(Oh-hi-yoe go-zie-mahss)

Good afternoon
Konnichi wa
(Kone-nee-chee wah)

Good evening
Komban wa
(Kome-bahn wah)

Good night
Oyasumi nasai
(Oh-yah-sue-me nah-sie)

How are you?
Ogenki desu ka?
(Oh-gane-kee dess kah?)

Goodbye
Sayonara*
(Sah-yoe-nah-rah)
*This poetic word literally means "If it must be so" (we part).

Take care (stay well)
Ogenki de
(Oh-gane-kee day)

Common Expressions

Thank you (standard speech)
Domo arigato
(Doe-moe ah-ree-gah-toe)

Thank you (polite speech)
Domo arigato gozaimasu
(Doe-moe ah-ree-gah-toe go-zie-mahss)

Excuse me (to attract attention)
Sumimasen
(Sue-me-mah-sin)

Excuse me (when interrupting or walking away from someone)
Shitsurei shimasu
(She-t'sue-ray-ee she-mahss)

Excuse me (when apologizing)
Sumimasen or *Gomen nasai*
(Sue-me-mah-sin / Go-mane nah-sie)

I'm sorry (apology)
Gomen nasai or *Sumimasen*
(Go-mane nah-sie / Sue-me-mah-sin)

I'm sorry / I have no excuse (a strong apology)
Moshi wake nai
(Moe-she wah-kay nie)

Excuse me / pardon me, but . . .
Sumimasen ga
(Sue-me-mah-sin gah)

Pardon me, but are you lost?
Sumimasen ga, michi ni mayoimashita ka?
(Sue-me-mah-sin gah, me-chee nee mah-yoe-ee-mah-sshta
kah?)

Please (do something)
Dozo or *Onegaishimasu*
(Doe-zoe / Oh-nay-guy-she-mahss)

That's (it's) all right
Daijobu desu
(Diejoe-buu dess)

Never mind
Kamaimasen
(Kah-my-mah-sin)

Please wait just a moment
Chotto omachi kudasai
(Choat-toe oh-mah-chee kuu-dah-sie)

You're welcome (don't mention it)
Do itashi mashite
(Doh ee-tah-she mah-ssh'tay)

Do you understand?
Wakarimasu ka?
(Wah-kah-ree-mahss kah?)

Do you speak English?
Eigo wo hanashimasu ka?
(Eh-ee-go oh hah-nah-she-mahss kah?)

I speak only a little Japanese
Watakushi wa Nihongo wo honno sukoshi hanasemasu
(Wah-tock-she wah Nee-hone-go oh hone-no suu-koe-she hah-nah-say-mahss)

Please speak slowly
Yukkuri hanashite kudasai
(Yuke-kuu-ree hah-nah-ssh'tay kuu-dah-sie)

I do not understand / I do not know
Wakarimasen
(Wah-kah-ree-mah-sin)

Making Your Own Sentences

To go beyond memorizing one- and two-word expressions, and to get the most out of this book, it is necessary for you to know how to construct your own basic sentences from the key words that follow.

As mentioned earlier, the grammatical order of the parts of speech in Japanese is subject-object-verb. This may sound (and feel) awkward at first, particularly if you begin comparing Japanese and English sentences word for word. So the point is don't compare them. Just accept the fact that Japanese has one structure and English has another, and both make sense.

It is / There is / There are / To have

Let's first look at Japanese verbs because they are the words that bring action/ movement to a sentence and determine whether it is positive or negative or in the present, past or future tense, etc.

There are two Japanese words for the very important verb "to be"—*desu* (dess), which is the common term, and *de gozaimasu* (day go-zie-mahss), which is the polite, honorific form. These words incorporate the meanings "I am, he/she/it is; we/you/they are."

The negative of *desu* (it isn't) is *de wa arimasen* (day wah ah-ree-mah sin), which in common, colloquial speech is generally shortened to *ja nai* (jah nie). The past tense of *desu* is *deshita* (desh-tah). The past tense of *de wa arimasen* is *de wa arimasen deshita* (day wah ah-ree-mah-sin desh-tah).

"There is/there are" in Japanese is *ga arimasu* (gah ah-ree-mahss) or *wa arimasu* (wah ah-ree-mahss) depending on the context. "There isn't/there aren't" is *ga arimasen* (gah ah-ree-mah-sin), etc. The past tense of *ga arimasu* is *ga arimasen deshita* (gah ah-ree-mah-sin desh-tah).

What might be called the third foundation verb, "to have," is expressed in Japanese by *motte imasu* (moat-tay ee-mahss). *Motte* means "having" or "holding," and *imasu* means "am," "is" or "are." The negative of *motte imasu* is *motte imasen* (moat-tay ee-mah-sin). The past tense is *motte imasen deshita* (moat-tay ee-mah-sin desh-tah).

Doing Without A's, The's & Plurals

As already noted, there is no definite or indefinite article (the/a) in Japanese, and very few plural forms. *Onna* (own-nah), for example, may mean woman, women, a woman or the women, depending on the context.

Kuruma (kuu-rue-mah) may mean car, cars, a car or the car, and so on. The word for you, *anata* (ah-nah-tah), may be expressed in the plural sense by adding the suffix *tachi* (tah-chee) or *gata* (gah-tah)—*anata-tachi* (ah-nah-tah-tah-chee), *anata-gata* (ah-nah-tahgah-tah). But this use is rare.

Asking Questions

Questions are formed in Japanese by adding *ka* (kah) at the end of words and sentences. In writing, *ka* takes the place of the English question mark (?). In speaking, *ka* is generally pronounced with little or no change in inflection. However, when speaking in a forceful manner, kah may be emphasized with appropriate degrees of passion.

Because the syllable *ka* is very common in ordinary Japanese words, I have chosen to include the question mark (?) following the *ka* at the end of questions in order to make the indication clearer. Here are the most common interrogative words and examples of their use:

Where - *doko* (doe-koe)

Where is / where are
Doko desu ka?
(Doe-koh dess kah?)

When - *itsu* (eet-sue)

When are you going?
Itsu ikimasu ka?
(Eet-sue ee-kee-mahss kah?)

What - *nani* (nah-nee)

What would you like to have?
Nani wo itashimashoka?
(Nah-nee oh ee-tah-she-mah-show kah?

Which - *dochira* (doe-chee-rah)

Which one would you like?
Dochira ga ii desu ka?
(Doe-chee-rah gah ee dess kah?)

Who - *donata* (doe-nah-tah)

Who is waiting for a taxi?
Takushi wo matte iru kata ga donata desho ka?
(Tahk-she oh mot-tay ee-rue kah-tah ga doe-nah-tah day-show kah?)

Whose - *donata-no* (doe-nah-tah-no)

Whose briefcase is this?
Kono kaban ga donata no desu ka?
(Koe-no kah-bahn gah doe-nah-tah no dess kah?)

Why - *doshite* (doe-sshtay)

Why aren't you going?
Doshite ikimasen ka?
(Doe-sshtay ee-kee-mah-sin kah?)

LEAVING THINGS OUT

One of the most interesting and useful characteristics of conversational Japanese is that the subject as well as the object are frequently left out in ordinary speech because both are subsumed within the verb form. In other words, Japanese verbs are commonly (and correctly!) used as complete sentences.

Knowledge of just a few dozen Japanese verbs and adjectives makes it possible for you to express over a hundred key concepts, and communicate the thoughts clearly.

For example, the Japanese word for "go" is *ikimasu* (ee-kee-mahss). This word, all by itself, is used to mean: I am going, we are going, he/she is going, they are going--with the meaning understood by the context. The same term also means "will go." Using the past, future and other forms of the same word you can express around a dozen variations of the term "go."

Here are some of the other commonly used forms of *ikimasu*.

Ikimasen (ee-kee-mah-sin)
I am not going; he/she is not going; we/they are not going.

Ikitai (ee-kee-tie)
I/we/they want to go; he/she wants to go.

Ikimashita (ee-kee-mah-sshtah)
I/helshe/we/they went.

Ikimasen deshita (ee-kee-mah-sin desh-tah)
I/he/she/we/they didn't go.

Ikimasu ka? (ee-kee-mahss kah?)
Are you/we/they going? Is he/she going?

Ikimasen ka? (ee-kee-mah-sin kah?)
Aren't you/we/they going? Isn't he/she going?

Ikimashita ka (ee-kee-mah-sshtah kah?)
Did you/he/she/they go?

The full Japanese equivalent of "Are you going?" is *Anata wa ikimasu ka?* (Ah-nah-tah wah ee-kee-mahss kah?), but the *anata wa* is generally dropped unless there is reason to emphasize "you."

Here are some other key Japanese verbs, all of which, in their various grammatical forms, can be used as complete sentences, like *ikimasu*:

Tabemasu (tah-bay-mahss)
I will/am going to eat; he/she will/is going to eat; we/they will/are going to eat.

Tabemasen (tah-bay-mah-sin)
I am not going to eat; he/she is not going to eat; we/they are not going to eat.

Tabetai (tah-bay-tie)
I/we/they want to eat; he/she wants to eat.

Tabemashita (tah-bay-mah-sshtah)
I/he/she/they/we ate.

Tabemasen deshita (tah-bay-mah-sin desh-tah)
I/we/she/he/they did not eat.

Tabemasu ka? (tah-bay mahss kah?)
Are you/we/they going to eat? Is he/she going to eat?

Tabemasen ka (tah-bay-mah-sin kah?)
Aren't you/we/they going to eat? Isn't he/she going to eat?

Tabemashita ka? (tah-bay-mah-sshtah kah?)
Did you/he/she/they eat?

Nomimasu (no-me-mahss)
I am going to drink; we/they are going to drink; he/she is going to drink.

Nomimasen (no-me-mah-sin)

I am not going to/will not/do not drink; he/she is not going to/will not/does not drink; we/they are not going to/will not/do not drink.

Nomitai (no-me-tie)
I/we/they want to drink; he/she wants to drink.

Nomimashita (no-me-mah-sshtah)
I/he/she/we/they drank.

Nomimasen deshita (no-me-mah-sin-desh-tah)
I/he/she/we/they did not drink.

Nomimasu ka? (no-me-mahss kah?)
Are you/they/we going to drink; is he/she going to drink? [This is also used in the sense of "do you/they want to drink?]

Nomimasen ka? (no-me-mah-sin kah?)
Aren't you/they/we going to drink? Isn't he/she going to drink?

No*mimashita ka?* (no-me-mah-sshtah kah?)
Did you/he/she/they drink?

Note that these three example verbs (*ikimasu, tabemasu, nomimasu*), and the ones following, have the same ending suffix, masu (mahss). They all conjugate exactly the same way and are used in the same way.

Wakarimasu (wah-kah-ree-mahss) - understand:
wakarimasen, wakaritai, wakarimashita, wakarimasen deshita, wakarimasu ka.~ wakarimasen ka?, wakarimashita ka?

Mimasu (me-mahss) - see:
mimasen; mitai, mimashita, mimasen deshita, mimasu ka?, mimasen ka?, mimashita ka?

Kikimasu (kee-kee-mahss) - hear:
kikimasen, kikitai, kikimashita, kikimasen deshita, kikimasen ka?, kikimashita ka?

Hanashimasu (hah-nah-she-mahss) speak:
hanashimasen, hanashitai, hanashimashita, hanashimasen deshita, hanashimasen ka? hanashimashita ka?

Kaimasu (kie-mahss) buy:
kaimasen, kaitai, kaimashita, kaimasen deshita. kaimasen ka?

kaimashita ka?

Arukimasu (ah-rue-kee-mahss) - walk:
arukimasen, arukitai, arukimashita arukimasen deshita,
arukimasen ka? arukimashita ka?

Kakimasu (kah-kee-mahss) - write:
kakimasen, kakitai, kakimashita, kakimasen deshita, kakimasen
ka?, kakimashita ka?

Demasu (day-mahss) - go out:
demasen, detai, demashita, demasen deshita, demasen ka?,
demashita ka?

Meeting People

My name is_____
Watakushi no namae wa_____desu
(Wah-tock-she no nah-my wah _____ dess)

What is your name?
Anata no namae wa nan desu ka?
(Ah-nah-tah no nah-my wah nahn dess kah?)

I'm pleased to meet you
Hajimete o'me ni kakarimasu
(Hahjee-may-tay oh-may nee kah-kah-ree-mahss)

or the more colloquial:
How do you do
Hajimemashite, dozo yoroshiku
(Hah-jee-may-mah-ssh'tay, doe-zoe yoe-roe-ssh'kuu)

What is his/her name?
Anohito no namae wa nan desu ka?
(Ah-no-ssh-toe no nah-my wah nahn dess kah?)

This is Mr./Mrs./Miss
Kochira wa San desu
(Koe-chee-rah wah Sahn dess)

Yes and No

"Yes" in Japanese is *hai* (hi) and "no" is *iie* (ee-eh). But these words are not used as often in Japanese as they are in English. It is more common in Japanese to use the positive and negative forms of verbs to express the idea of "yes" and "no."

For example, instead of answering "yes" or "no" to the question, "Are you going?", the typical Japanese response is *ikimasu* (ee-kee-mahss) "I'm going," or *ikimasen* (ee-kee-mah-sin) "I'm not going."

However, *hai* and *iie* are perfectly understandable in this and similar situations, and may be used without breaching any etiquette.

Beware of asking negative questions of the Japanese. Their answer to a negative question is the opposite of what it is in English. In other words, their response to *ikimasen ka* (ee-kee-mah-sin kah?)—"Aren't you going?"—is *Hai*—"yes," meaning "I'm not going."

Or, a fuller response may be, *Hai, ikimasen*—"Yes, I'm not going"—in which case, the meaning may be clearer to those conditioned to English.

Honorifics

The Japanese are well-known for their formal, stylized etiquette in both speech and physical behavior. The use of honorifics in speech is an important part of their social etiquette, and is a conspicuous sign of one's education and standards.

Probably the most commonly use honorifics are *o* and *go* placed before nouns and verbs to indicate politeness and respect. One of the best known examples is the *o* prefixed to *sake* (sah-kay), Japan's famous wine-like drink brewed from rice: *o-sake* (oh-sah-kay). The reason for attaching an honorific to *sake* probably evolved from the fact that it was originally drunk as part of sacred Shinto rituals.

Prefixing *o* to such words as "friend" (*o-tomodachi* (oh-toe-moe-dah chee) and "house" (*o-taku* / oh-tah-kuu), is a very polite way of referring to "your friend," "your house."

The difference between the use of *o* and *go* is tricky for the newcomer to Japanese. *O* is generally prefixed only to words that are Japanese in origin, while *go* is usually prefixed only to words of Chinese origin. The only practical way of dealing with this difference is to not use either one until you hear it used or learn it from some reliable text.

The Guest as King or Queen

Guest - *o'kyaku* (oh-k'yah-kuu)

This is one of the most important words in the Japanese language and in Japanese culture as a whole. The Japanese have been conditioned for centuries to address personal guests with special courtesy and extend extraordinary service and hospitality to them. This tradition has weakened significantly since the introduction of Western ways into Japan, but enough of it remains to set the Japanese apart.

Business customers, including airline passengers, are also regularly referred to as *okyaku*, and are generally treated with the respect and special care that one extends to valued guests in one's home.

Okyaku, with the honorific *San* (sahn) attached, is commonly used by itself as a kind of title when clerks and others in service industries address customers or clients, particularly when they don't know their names. In other words, instead of using "Sir" or "Madame" or "you," the Japanese way is to use *Okyaku San*— "Mr. (Mrs. or Miss) Guest."

When dealing with large numbers of Japanese visitors, it is virtually impossible to remember all of their names, even after two or three days, so being able to take advantage of the custom of using okyaku as a tide makes it possible for you to be totally correct in the deepest cultural sense whenever you address anyone for any purpose. Just be sure you add the honorific *san* (sahn) to it.

Basic Building Blocks
of Japanese

Using Numbers

Being able to use numbers is one of the primary keys to communicating in any language, on even the most basic level. I recommend that you spend extra time on learning how to count in Japanese, and how to use numbers in conjunction with days, months, years, time, people, and things in general.

There are two counting systems in Japanese, one that goes only from one through ten, and a second system that begins with one and goes all the way up. The former is a native Japanese system. The latter was imported from China nearly two thousand years ago.

The Japanese system is used for counting small things that are odd-shaped and do not fit into any traditional, precise category of things (such as hamburgers, or pieces of pie or cake), and for designating one person or two people. In practically all other cases, the Chinese system is used.

The Cardinal Numbers

Japanese	Chinese
1 hitotsu (ssh-tote-sue)	ichi (ee-chee)
2 futatsu (fuu-tot-sue)	ni (nee)
3 mittsu (meet-sue)	san (sahn)
4 yottsu (yote-sue)	shi, yo, yon (she, yoe, yoan)
5 itsutsu (ee-t'sue-t'sue)	go (go)
6 muttsu (moot-sue)	roku (roe-kuu)
7 nanatsu (nah-nah-t'sue)	shichi (she-chee)
8 yattsu (yaht-sue)	hachi (hah-chee)
9 kokonotsu (koe-koe-note-sue)	ku, kyu (kuu, que)
10 to (toe)	ju (juu)

From 10 on, only the Chinese numbers are used. Note that they are combinations of 10 and multiples of 10 plus 1 thru 9, with special words for 100, 1,000, 10,000, etc.

11 - ju-ichi (juu-ee-chee)
12 - ju-ni (juu-nee)
13 - ju-san (juu-sahn)
14 - u-yon (juu-yoan)
15 - ju-go (juu-go)
16 - ju-roku (juu-roe-kuu)
17 - ju-shichi,ju-nana (juu-she-chee,juu-nah-nah)
18 - ju-hachi (juu-hah-chee)
19 - ju-ku,jukyu (juu-kuu,juu-que)
20 - ni-ju (nee-juu)
21 - ni-ju-ichi (neejuu-ee-chee)
22 - ni-ju-ni (neejuu-nee)
23 - ni-ju-san (neejuu-sahn)
24 - niju-yon (neejuu-yoan)
25 - niju-go (neejuu-go)
26 - niju-roku (nee-juu-roe-kuu)
27 - niju-shichi, niju-nana (neejuu-she-chee, nee-juu-nah-nah)

28 - ni-ju-hachi (neejuu-hah-chee)
29 - niju-ku, ni-ju-kyu (nee-juu-kuu, nee-juu-que)
30 - san-ju (sahnjuu)
40 - yonju (yoanjuu)
50 - go-ju (gojuu)
60 - rokuju (roe-kuujuu)
70 - nana-ju (nah-nahjuu)
80 - hachi-ju (hah-chee-juu)
90 - kyuju (quejuu)
100 - hyaku (h'yah-kuu)
101 - hyaku-ichi (h'yah-kuu-ee-chee)
102 - hyaku-ni (h'yah-kuu-nee)
103 - hyaku-san (h'yah-kuu-sahn)
110 - hyaku-ju (h'yah-kuu-juu)
111 - hyaku-ju-ichi (h'yah-kukjuu-ee-chee)
120 - hyaku-niju (h'yah-ku-neejuu)
121 - hyaku-ni-ju-ichi (h'yah-kuu-neejuu-ee-chee)
130 - hyaku-sanju (h'yah-kuu-sahnjuu)
140 - hyaku-yonjuu (h'yah-kuu-yoanjuu)
200 - ni-hyaku (nee-h'yah-kuu)
300 - sam-6yaku (sahm-b'yah-kuu)
400 - yon-hyaku (yoan-h'yah-kuu)
500 - go-hyaku (go-h'yah-kuu)
600 - rop-pyaku (rope-p'yah-kuu)
700 - nana-hyaku (nah-nah-h'yah-kuu)
800 - hap-pyaku (hop-p'yah-kuu)
900 - kyu-hyaku (que-h'yah-kuu)
1000 - sen or issen (sin / ees-sin)
1500 - sen-go-hyaku (sin-go-h'yah-kuu)
1550 - sen-go-hyaku-go-ju (sin-go-h'yah-kuu-gojuu)
2000 - ni-sen (nee-sin)
3000 - san-zen (sahn-zen)
4000 - yon-sen (yoan-sin)
5000 - go-sen (go-sin)
6000 - roku-sen (roe-kuu-sin)
7000 - nana-sen (nah-nah-sin)
8000 - has-sen (hahs-sin)
9000 - kyu-sen (que-sin)
10,000 - ichi-man (ee-chee-mahn)
11,000 - ichi-man-issen (ee-chee-mahn-ees-sin)
20,000 - ni-man (nee-mahn)
50,000 - go-man (go-mahn)
100,000 - ju-man (juu-mahn)
200,000 - ni ju-man (neejuu-mahn)
500,000 - go-ju-man (gojuu-mahn)
1,000,000 - hyaku-man (h'yah-kuu-mahn)

5,000,000 - go-hyaku-man (go-h'yah-kuu-mahn)

Time of Day

The Japanese word for "hour" or "o'clock" is *ji* (jee). This, combined with the appropriate number, makes up the hours of the day:

1 o'dock - ichi-ji (ee-chee jee)
2 o'clock - ni ji (nee jee)
3 o'clock - san ji (sahn jee)
4 o'clock - yo ji (yoe jee)
5 o'dock - go ji (go jee)
6 o'clock - roku ji (roe-kuu jee)
7 o'clock - shichi ji (she-chee jee)
8 o'clock - hachi ji (hah-chee jee)
9 o'clock - ku ji (kuu jee)
10 o'clock - ju ji (juu jee)
11 o'clock - ju-ichi ji (juu-ee-chee jee)
12 o'clock - ju-ni jee (juu-nee jee)

Half (past) - han (hahn)

Half past one
ichi ji han
(ee-chee-jee hahn)

2:30
ni ji han
(nee-jee hahn)

"Minute" in Japanese is either *pun* (poon) or *hun* (hoon), depending on the phonetics of the number before it.

1 minute - ip pun (eep-poon)
2 minutes - ni hun (nee hoon)
3 minutes - san pun (sahn poon)
4 minutes - yon pun (yoan poon)
5 minutes - go hun (go hoon)
6 minutes - rop pun (rope poon)
7 minutes - nana hun (nah-nah hoon)
8 minutes - hachi hun (hah-chee hoon)
9 minutes - kyu hun (que hoon)
10 minutes - jip pun (jeep poon)
11 minutes - ju-ip pun (juu-eep poon)

12 minutes - ju-ni hun (juu-nee hoon)
13 minutes - ju-san pun (juu-sahn poon)
14 minutes - ju-yon pun (juu-yoan poon)
15 minutes - ju-go hun (juu-go hoon)
20 minutes - ni-jip pun (neejeep poon)
25 minutes - ni-ju-go hun (neejuu-go hoon)
30 minutes - san-jip pun (sahnjeep poon)
40 minutes - yon-jip pun (yoanjeep poon)
50 minutes - go-jip pun (go-jeep poon)

Before - *mae* (my)
After - *tsugi* (t'sue-ghee)

Five minutes before one o'clock
Ichi ji go hun mae
(Ee-chee jee go hoon my)

Five minutes after one o'clock
Ichi ji go hun tsugi
(Ee-chee jee go hoon t'sue-ghee)

Ten minutes to twelve
Ju-ni ji jip pun mae
auu-nee jee jeep poon my)

Twenty minutes past nine
Ku ji ni-jip pun tsugi
(Kuu ji neejeep poon t'sue-ghee)

Quarter to nine
Ku ji ju-go hun mae
(Kuu jee juu-go hoon my)

Special "Counters"

Another special feature of the Japanese way of counting is the use of some thirty category designators or counters that correspond to the English use of "head" when talking about six head of cattle or horses. Several of these counters undergo changes in pronunciation (and spelling), depending on the words that precede them. But they remain easily recognizable. Among the most commonly used of these numeratives are:

mai (my) for flat things such as paper, pieces of cloth, boards, etc.

hon/bon (hoan/bone), used in counting round, long objects such as pens, bottles, legs, needles, ropes, tubes, etc.

hai/pai (hi/pie) to designate glasses or cups of liquids.

satsu (sotsue), for counting books; hiki (he-kee) for counting animals, fish and insects.

nin (neen) for counting people.

ji (jee) for hours of the day.

kire (kee-rayj for counting slices of cake, meat, etc.

ko (koe) for counting items with indiscriminate shapes, and so on.

Some examples:

1 sheet of paper - *kami ichi-mai* (kah-me ee-chee-my)
2 sheets of paper - *kami ni-mai* (kah-me nee-my)
3 sheets of paper - *kami san-mai* (kah-me sahn-my)

1 bottle - *bin ippon* (bean eep-pone)
2 bottles - *bin ni-hon* (bean nee-hoan)
3 bottles - *bin san-bon* (bean sahn-bone)

The "counter" for houses or buildings (which is very useful in giving directions) is *ken* (kane): one building – *ik ken* (eek-kane); two buildings – *ni ken* (nee kane); three houses – *san ken* (sahn kane).

Days

Monday - *getsuyobi* (gates-yoe-bee)
Tuesday - *kayobi* (kah-yoe-bee)
Wednesday - *suiyobi* (suu-ee -yoe-bee)
Thursday - *mokuyobi* (moe-kuu-yoe-bee)
Friday - *kinyobi* (keen-yoe-bee)
Saturday - *doyobi* (doe-yoe-bee)
Sunday - *nichiyobi* (nee-chee-yoe-bee)

Today - *kyo* (k'yoe)
Tomorrow - *ashita* (ah-sshtah)
Day after tomorrow - *asatte* (ah-sot-tay)
Yesterday - *kino* (kee-noh)
Day before yesterday - *ototoi* (oh-toe-toy)

Morning - *asa* (ah-sah)
This morning - *kesa* (kay-sah)
Before noon (A.M.) - *go zen* (go zen)

Noon (around noon) - *hiru* (he-rue)
Afternoon (P.M.) - *gogo* (go go)
Evening - *ban* (bahn); *yugata* (yuu-gah-tah)
This evening- *kon ban* (kone bahn)
Night – *yoru* (yoe-rue)
Tonight - *kon* ya (kone yah)

Weekdays - *hei-jitsu* (hay-eejeet-sue)
Sundays and holidays - *kyu-jitsu* (que-jeet-sue)

Days by the Number

one day - ichi nichi (ee-chee nee-chee)
two days - hutsuka kan (who-t'sue kah kahn)
three days - mikka kan (meek-kah kahn)
four days - yokka kan (yoke-kah kahn)
five days - itsuka kan (ee-t'sue kah kahn)
six days - muika kan (moo-ee kah kahn)
seven days - nanoka kan (nah-no kah kahn)
eight days - youka kan (yoe-oh kah kahn)
nine days - kokono ka kan (koe-koe-no kah kahn)
ten days - touka kan (toe-kah kahn)
eleven days - ju-ichi nichi kan (juu ee-chee nee-chee kahn)
twelve days - ju-ni nichi kan (juu nee nee-chee kahn)

Weeks

One week - is shukan (ees shuu-kahn)
Two weeks - ni shukan (nee shuu-kahn)
Three weeks - san shukan (sahn shuu-kahn)
Four weeks - yon shukan (yoan shuu-kahn)
Five weeks - go shukan (go shuu-kahn)
Six weeks - roku shukan (roe-kuu shuu-kahn)
This week - kon shu (kone shuu)
Next week - rai shu (rye shuu)

Week after next - *sa rai shu* (sah rye shuu)
Last week - *sen shu* (sane shuu)
Week before last - *sen sen shu* (sane sane shuu)

Months

The Japanese names for the months are combinations of the word *gatsu* (got-sue), which literally means "moon," and the numbers 1 through 12 (first month, second month, etc.).

January- ichigatsu (ee-chee-got-sue)
February - nigatsu (nee-got-sue)
March - sangatsu (sahn-got-sue)
April - shigatsu (she-got-sue)
May - gogatsu (go-got-sue)
June - rokugatsu (roe-kuu-got-sue)
July- shichigatsu (she-chee-got-sue)
August - hachigatsu (hah-chee-got-sue)
September - kugatsu (kuu-got-sue)
October - jugatsu (juu-got-sue)
November - juichigatsu (juu-ee-chee-got-sue)
December - junigatsu (juu-nee-got-sue)

The "counter" for months is ka (kah) in combination with getsu (gate-sue), the general word for "month."

One month - ikka getsu (eek-kah gate-sue)
Two months - nikka getsu (neek-kah gate-sue)
Three months - sanka getsu (sahn-kah gate-sue)
Four months - yonka getsu (yoan-kah gate-sue)
Five months - goka getsu (go-kah gate-sue)
Six months - rokka getsu (roke-kah gate-sue)

This month - kon getsu (kone gate-sue)
Next month - rai getsu (rye gate-sue)
Month after next - sa rai getsu (sah rye gate-sue)
Last month - sen getsu (sane gate-sue)
Month before last - sen sen getsu (sane sane gate-sue)

Years

One year - ichi nen kan (ee-chee nane kahn)
Two years - ni nen kan (nee nane kahn)
Three years - san nen kan (sahn nane kahn)
Four years - yon nen kan (yoan nane kahn)
Five years - go nen kan (go nane kahn)

This year - kotoshi (koe-toe-she)
Next year - rai nen (rye nane)
Last year - kyo nen (k'yoe nane)

Days of the Month

There is a special word for the first day of the month and for the 20th day. From the second day to the tenth day, the Japanese system of numbers is used in conjunction with the suffix *ka* (kah), which is another way of saying "day." From the 11th day on, the Chinese system of numbers is used in conjunction with *nichi* (nee-chee), which also means "day," with the exception of the 14th and 24th days, which revert back to the Japanese system.

1st day of the month - tsuitachi (t'sue-ee-tah-chee)
2nd day of the month - futsuka (futes-kah)
3rd day of the month - mikka (meek-kah)
4th day of the month - yokka (yoke-kah)
5th day of the month - itsuka (eet-sue-kah)
6th day of the month - muika (muu-ee-kah)
7th day of the month - nanoka (nah-no-kah)
8th day of the month - yoka (yoh-kah)
9th day of the month - kokonoka (koe-koe-no-kah)
10th day of the month - toka (toe-kah)
11th day of the month - ju-ichi nichi (juu-ee-chee nee-chee)
12th day of the month - ju-ni nichi (juu-nee nee-chee)
13th day of the month - ju-san nichi (juu-sahn nee-chee)
14th day of the month - ju-yokka (juu-yoke-kah)
15th day of the month - ju-go nichi (juu-go nee-chee)
16th day of the month - ju-roku nichi (juu-roe-kuu nee-chee)
17th day of the month - ju-shichi nichi (juu-she-chee nee-chee)
18th day of the month - ju-hachi nichi (juu-hah-chee nee-chee)
19th day of the month - ju-ku nichi (juu-kuu nee-chee)
20th day of the month - niju nichi (neejuu nee-chee); hatsu ka (hot-sue kah)*

*Hatsuka is a special word often used for the 20th day of the month instead of niju nichi

21st day of the month - niju-ichi nichi (ne-juu-ee-chee nee-chee)
22nd day of the month - ni ju-ni nichi (nee-juu-nee nee-chee)
23rd day of the month - niju-san nichi (nee-juu-sahn nee-chee)
24th day of the month - ni ju-yok ka (nee-juu-yoke kah)
25th day of the month - ni ju-go nichi (nee-juu-go nee-chee)
26th day of the month - ni ju-roku nichi (nee-juu-roe-kuu nee-chee)
27th day of the month - ni ju-shichi nichi (neejuu-she-chee nee-chee)
28th day of the month - ni ju-hachi nichi (nee-juu-hah-chee nee-chee)
29th day of the month - ni ju-ku nichi (nee-juu-kuu nee-chee)
30th day of the month - san ju nichi (sahn-juu nee-chee)

31st day of the month - san ju-ichi nichi (sahn-juu-ee-chee nee-chee)

The Ordinal Numbers

The ordinal numbers in Japanese are made by combining *bamme* (bahm-may) with the appropriate cardinal number:

1st - ichi-bamme (ee-chee-bahm-may)
2nd - ni-bamme (nee-bahm-may)
3rd - san-bamme (sahn-bahm-may)
4th - yon-bamme (yoan-bahm-may)
5th - go-bamme (go-bahm-may)
10th - ju-bamme (juu-bahm-may)
15th - ju-go-bamme (juu-go-bahm-may)
100th - hyaku-bamme (h'yah-kuu-bahm-may)

The Seasons

Spring - *haru* (hah-rue)
Summer - *natsu* (not-sue)
Fall - *aki* (ah-kee)
Winter - *fuyu* (fuu-yuu)

The Weather

Weather - *tenki* (tane-kee)
Good weather - *ii otenki* (ee oh-tane-kee)
Bad weather - *warui otenki* (wah-rue-ee oh-tane-kee)

The weather is nice today, isn't it!
Kyo wa ii otenki desu, ne!
(K'yoe wah ee oh-tane-kee dess, nay!)

The weather will be better tomorrow
Ashita no otenki wa yoku narimasu
(Ah-sshtah no oh-tane-kee wah yoe-kuu nah-ree-mahss)

The weather will be bad tomorrow
Ainiku, ashita no otenki wa waruku narimasu
(Aye-nee-kuu, ah-sshtah no oh-tane-kee wah wah-rue-kuu nah-ree-mahss)

Climate - *kiko* (kee-koe)
Rain - *ame* (ah-may)

To rain - *ame ga furimasu* (ah-may gah fuu-ree-mahss)
It's raining - *ame ga fuitte imasu* (ah-may ga fuu-ee-tay ee-mahss)
Wind - *kaze* (kah-zay)
It's windy - *kaze ga fuitte imasu* (kah-zay gah fuu-ee-tay ee-mahss)
Clouds - *kumo* (kuu-moe)
It's cloudy - *kumotte imasu* (kuu-moat-tay ee-mahss)
Fog - *kiri* (kee-ree)
It's foggy - *kiri shite imasu* (kee-ree sshtay ee-mahss)
Temperature - *kion* (kee-own); ondo (own-doe)

The temperature today is going to be about 20 degrees (C.)
Kyo no ondo wa daitai niju do ni narimasu
(K'yoe no own-doe wah die-tie nee-juu doh nee nah-ree-mahss)

Centigrade, Celsius - *sesshi* (say-sshe)
Fahrenheit - *kasshi* (kahs-she)
Thermometer - *kandankei* (kahn-dahn-kay-ee)
Hot - *atsui* (aht-sue-ee)

Today is really hot!
Kyo wa honto ni atsui desu!
(K'yoe wah hoan-toe nee aht-sue-ee dess!)

Cold - *samui* (sah-muu-ee)

It will be cold tonight
Komban samuku narimasu
(Kome-bahn sah-muu-kuu nah-ree-mahss)

Warm - atatakai (ah-tah-tah-kie)
Humid (and hot) - *mushi-atsui* (muu-shee-aht-sue-e)
Humidity - shimerike (she-may-ree-kay)

The humidity is high
Shimerike ga takai desu
(She-may-ree-kay ~ah tah-kie dess)

Sun - *hi* (he); *taiyo* (tie-yoe)
Sunny day - *uraraka-na hi* (uu-rah-rah-kah-nah he)

The sun is shining
Hi ga kagayaite imasu
(He gah kah-gah-yie-tay ee-mahss)

The Telephone

Hello - *moshi-moshi* (moe-she moe-she)*

*This is a special word used only on the telephone or when trying to attract someone's attention, as when calling out, "Excuse me!"

Telephone - *denwa* (dane-wah)
Telephone operator - *kokanshu* (koe-kahn-shuu)
Telephone book - *denwa cho* (dane-wah choe)
English-language telephone book - *Eigo no denwa cho* (Eh-ee-go no dane wah choe)
Japanese-language telephone book - *Nihongo no denwa cho* (Nee-hoan-go no dane-wah choe)
Telephone (make a call) - *denwa wo kakemasu* (dane-wah oh kah-kay mahss)
Telephone call - *denwa* (dane-wah)
Telephone number - *denwa bango* (dane-wah bahn-go)
Long-distance call - *chokyori denwa* (choe-k'yoe-ree dane-wah)
International phone call - *kokusai denwa* (koke-sie dane-wah)
Local call - *shinai no denwa* (she-nie no dane-wah)
Collect call - *ryokin senpo barai no denwa* (r'yoe-keen sen-poe bah-rye no dane-wah)
Person-to-person call - *pasonaru koru* (pah-soe-nah-rue koe-rue)
Busy - *hanasuchu* (hah-nah-suu-chuu)
The line is busy - *Hanasuchu desu* (Hah-nah-sue-chuu dess)
Return call - *koru bakku* (koe-rue bahk-kuu)

I will call you back in two or three minutes
Ni sanpun de koru bakku shimasu
(Nee sahn-poon day koe-rue bahk-kuu she-mahss)

House phone - *okunai denwa* (oh-kuu-nie dane-wah)

The house phones are in that corner
Okunai denwa ga sono sumi ni arimasu
(Oh-kuu-nie dane-wah gah so-no sue-me nee ah-ree-mahss)

Public phone - *koshu denwa* (koe-shuu dane-wah)

There is a public phone on the left side of the door
Koshu denwa ga doa no hidari gawa ni arimasu
(Koe-shuu dane-wah gah doe-ah no he-dah-ree gah-wah nee ah-ree-mahss)

Coin telephone - *koin no denwa* (koe-een no dane-wah)
Credit card phone - *kurejitto kado denwa* (kuu-ray-jeet-toe kah-doe danewah)
Telephone charge - *denwa dai* (dane-wah die)
Telephone extension - *naisen* (nie-sen)
Extension number - *naisen no bango* (nie-sen no bahn-go)
Message - *kotozuke* (koe-toe-zoo-kay); meseji (may-say-jee)

Mr./Miss/Mrs. Tanaka, there was a telephone call for you
Tanaka San, denwa ga arimashita
(Tah-nah-kah Sahn, dane-wah gah ah-ree-mah-sshtah)

There are no messages (for you)
Meseji ga arimasen
(May-say-jee gah ah-ree-mah-sin)

*The international telephone country code for Japan is 81. City codes (when calling Japan from abroad) include: Tokyo 3, Osaka 6, Kyoto 75, Yokohama 45, Nagoya 52, Kobe 78, and Sapporo 11.

Banks & Money

Authorized money-changer - *konin ryo-gaesho* (koe-neen r'yoe-guy-show)
Bank - *ginko* (gheen-koe)
Bank account number - *koza bango* (koe-zah bahn-go)
Bank branch - *ginko shiten* (gheen-koe she-tane)
Branch number - *ten go* (tane go)

Bank employee - *ginko in* (gheen-koe een)
Bill (paper money) - *shihei* (she-hay-ee); (when counting bills) *satsu* (sahtsue)

Are $100 bills all right?
Hyaku doru satsu wa yoroshii desu ka?
(H'yah-kuu doe-rue saht-sue wah yoe-roe-shee dess kah?)

Break a bill (into smaller units) - *komakaku shimasu* (koe-mah-kah-kuu she-mahss)

Cash - *genkin* (gane-keen)

Will you pay in cash?
Genkin de haraimasu ka?
(Gane-keen day hah-rye-mahss kah?)

ATM – *a-t-mu* (a-t-m-uu)
Cash card - *kyasshu kado* (k'yahs-shuu kah-doe)
Credit Card – *kurejjito kado* (kuu-ray-jeet-toh kah-doh)
Change (small money left over) - *otsur*i (oh-t'sue-ree)
Small money - *komakai okane* (koe-mah-kie oh-kah-nay)
Change dollars to yen - *doru wo en ni kaerimasu* (doe-rue oh inn nee kie-ree-mahss)
Change yen to dollars - *en wo doru ni kaerimasu* (inn oh doe-rue nee kie-ree-mahss)
Charge/fee - *ryokin* (r'yoe-keen)
Check - *kogitte* (koe-geet-tay)
Counter - *kaunta* (kah-oon-tah)
Deposit (money in bank) - *nyukin shimasu* (n'yuu-keen she-mahss)
Dollar - *doru* (doe-rue)
One hundred dollars - *hyaku doru* (h'yah-kuu doe-rue)
Five hundred dollars - *go-hyaku doru* (go-h'yah-kuu doe-rue)
One thousand dollars - *sen doru* (sen doe-rue)
Exchange rate - *kansan ritsu* (kahn-sahn reet-sue)
Foreign exchange - *gaikoku kawase* (guy-koe-kuu kah-wah-say)
Franc - *furanku* (fuu-rahn-kuu)
Interest - *rishi* (ree-she)
Lira - *rira* (ree-rah)
Mark - *maruku* (mah-rue-kuu)
Money - *okane* (oh-kah-nay)
Money card - *mane kado* (mah-nay kah-doe)
Pound - *pondo* (pone-doe)
Refund - *haraimodosh*i (hah-rye-moe-doe-she)
Remittance - *sokin* (soe-keen)
Remittance to a foreign country - *gaikoku sokin* (guy-koe-kuu so-keen)
Traveler's check - *ryokosha kogitte* (r'yoe-koe-shah koe-geet-tay)
Trust bank - *shintaku ginko* (sheen-tah-kuu gheen-goe)
Euro – *yuroh* (yuu-roh)
Withdraw money - *okane wo oroshimasu* (oh-kah-nay oh oh-roe-she-mahss)
Yen - *en* (in)

Post Offices & Mail

Post Office - *yubinkyoku* (yuu-bean-k'yoe-kuu)
Mail (letters, etc.) - *yubin* (yuu-bean)

To mail (something) - *yubin wo dashimasu* (yuu-bean oh dah-she-mahss)
Address - *jusho* (juu-show)

Please write your address here
Koko ni jusho wo kaite kudasai
(Koe-koe nee juu-show oh kie-tay kuu-dah-sie)

Addressee - *atena* (ah-tay-nah)
Address tag - *nifuda* (nee-fuu-dah)
Aerogram (air letter forms) - *koku-shokan* (koe-kuu-show-kahn)
Airmail - *kokubin* (koe-kuu-bean)
E-mail – i-meru (ee-may-ruu)
Commemorative stamps - *kinen kitte* (kee-nane keet-tay)
Customs declaration - *zeikan shinkoku* (zay-ee-kahn sheen-koe-kuu); *zeikan kokuchi sho* (zay-ee-kahn koe-kuu-chee show)
Envelope - *futo* (fuu-toe)
Express mail - *sokutatsu* (soe-kuu-tot-sue)
Fragile (article) - *kowaremono* (koe-wah-ray-moe-no)

Is there anything breakable in this (box, package)?
Kowaremono ga haitte imasu ka?
(Koe-wah-ray-moe-no gah hite-tay ee-mahss kah?)

Insurance - *hoken* (hoe-kane)
Insure - *hoken wo tsukemasu* (hoe-kane oh t'sue-kay-mahss)

Shall I insure this?
Kore wa hoken wo tsukemasho ka?
(Koe-ray wah hoe-kane oh t'sue-kay-mah-show kah?)

Letter - *tegami* (tay-gah-me)
Mail-drop (mailbox) - *posuto* (poe-stoe)
Mail (send) - *dashimasu* (dah-she-mahss)
Parcel post - *kozutsumi* (koe-zoot-sue-me)
Picture postcard - *e hagaki* (ay hah-gah-kee)
Postage - *yubinryo* (yuu-bean-r'yoe)
Postage stamps - *kitte* (keet-tay)
Post box - *yubin bako* (yuu-bean bah-koe)

There is a post box in the lobby of the hotel
Hoteru no robi ni yubin bako ga arimasu
(Hoe-tay-rue no roe-beenee yuu-bean bah-koe gah ah-ree-
mahss)

Post office - *yubinkyoku* (yuu-bean-k'yoe-kuu
Postal money order - *yubin futsu kawase* (yuu-bean fute-sue
kah-wah-say)
Postcard - *hagaki* (hah-gah-kee)
Printed matter - *insatsu butsu* (een-sot-sue boot-sue)
Registered mail - *kakitome* (kah-kee-tome-may)

Seamail - *funabin* (fuu-nah-bean)
Small packet - *kogata hosobutsu* (koe-gah-tah hoe-so-boot-sue)
Special delivery- *soku tatsu* (soe-kuu taht-sue)
Stamp - *kitte* (keet-tay)
Stationery store - *bunbogu ya* (boon-boe-guu yah)
Signed receipt (mail) - *haitatsu shomei-tsuki* (hi-tot-sue show-
may-eet-ski)
Weight - *mekata* (may-kah-tah)
Writing paper - *binsen* (bean-sen)
Zip code - *yubin bango* (yuu-bean bahn-go)

What is your zip code?
Yubin bango wa nan desu ka?
(Yuu-bean bahn-go wah nahn dess kah?)

Giving Directions

Direction - *hogaku* (hoe-gah-kuu)

It's in that direction
Sono hogaku desu
(So-no hoe-gah-kuu dess)

Go in that direction
Sono hogaku e itte kudasai
(Soe-no hoe-gah-kuu eh eet-tay kuu-dah-sie)

North - *kita* (kee-tah)
East - *higashi* (he-gah-she)
South - *minami* (me-nah-me)
West - *nishi* (nee-she)

Alley (narrow lane) - *roji* (roe-jee)

Behind - ushiro (uu-she-roe)
Beside, next to - *soba* (soe-bah)
Close-by - *sugu chikaku* (sue-guu chee-kah-kuu)
Corner - *kado* (kah-doe)
Dead-end (end of street) - *tsuki-atari* (t'ski-ah-tah-ree)
Diagonally opposite - *suji mukai* (sue-jee muu-kie)
Far - *toi* (toy)
Front - *mae* (my)
Intersection - *kosaten* (koe-sah-tane)
Landmark - *mejirushi* (may-jee-rue-she)
Left - *hidari* (he-dah-ree)
Near - *chikai* (chee-kie)

Next to - *tonari* (toe-nah-ree)
Opposite - *muko* (muu-koe)
Other side - *muko gawa* (muu-koe gah-wah)
Over there - *asoko* (ah-so-koe)
Parking garage/lot - *chusha jo* (chuu-shah joe)

Pedestrian Crossing - *oodan hodo* (ohh-dahn hoe-doe)
Railroad crossing - *fumikiri* (fuu-me-kee-ree)
Right (direction) - *migi* (mee-ghee)
Side road - *yoko michi* (yoe-koe me-chee)
Side street - *yoko cho* (yoe-koe choe)
Sign, signboard - *kanban* (kahn-bahn)
Straight - *massugu* (mahs-sue-guu)
Street - *michi* (me-chee); *dori* (doe-ree)
Street corner - *kado* (kah-doe)

First corner - *ichi-bamme no kado* (ee-chee-bahm-may no kah-doe)
Second corner - *ni-bamme no kado* (nee-bahm-may no kah-doe)
Third corner - *san-bamme no kado* (sahn-bahm-may no kah-doe)

There - *soko* (soe-koe)
This side - *kochira gawa* (koe-chee-rah gah-wah)
Traffic light (signal) - *shingo* (sheen-go)
Turn - *magarimasu* (mah-gah-ree-mahss)
Turn at the corner - *kado de magarimasu* (kah-doe day mah-gah-reemahss)
Turn back- *modorimasu* (moe-doe-ree-mahss)
Turn left - *hidari e magarimasu* (he-dah-ree eh mah-gah-ree-mahss)
Turn right - *migi e magarimasu* (me-ghee eh mah-gah-ree-mahss)

Turn right at the third corner - *San bamme no kado de migi e magatte kudasai*
(Sahn bahm-may no kah-doe day me-ghee eh mah-got-tay kuu-dah-sie)
Turn (curve) in the street/road- *michi no magari-kado* (mee-chee no mah-gah-ree kah-doe)

Distances

100 meters – *hyaku metoru* (h'yah-kuu may-toe-rue)
200 meters - *ni-hyaku metoru* (nee h'yah-kuu may-toe-rue)
300 meters - *sam-byaku metoru* (sahm-b'yah-kuu may-toe-rue)
Half a kilometer - *han kiro* (hahn kee-roe)
One kilometer - *ichi kiro* (ee-chee kee-roe)
Two kilometers - *ni kiro* (nee kee-roe)

Renting Cars

Car - *kuruma* (kuu-rue-mah); *jidosha* (jee-doe-shah); *ka* (kah)
Car park - *chusha jo* (chuu-shah joe)
Cash - *genkin* (gane-keen)
Charge per day - *ichi-nichi no ryokin* (ee-chee-nee-chee no r'yoe-keen)
Charge per week - *isshukan no ryokin* (ees-shuu-kahn no r'yoe-keen)
Charge for two weeks - *nishukan no ryokin* (nee-shuu-kahn no r'yoe-keen)
Charge per month - *ikkagetsukan no ryokin* (eek-kah-gate-sue-kahn no r'yoe-keen)
Condition - *choshi* (choe-she)
Bad condition - *choshi ga warui* (choe-she gah wah-rue-ee)
Good condition - *choshi ga ii* (choe-she gah ee)
Cost of gasoline - *gasorin dai* (gah-so-reen die)

The cost of the gasoline is included
Gasorin dai wa komi desu
(Gah-so-reen die wah koe-me dess)

Credit card - *kurejitto kado* (kuu-ray-jeet-toe kah-doe)
Deposit - *hoshokin* (hoe-show-keen)

A deposit is required
Hoshokin ga hitsuyo desu
(Hoe-show-keen gah heet-sue-yoe dess)

Destination - *mokutekichi* (moe-kuu-tay-kee-chee)

Dimmers - *dima* (dee-mah)
Driver's license - *unten menkyosho* (oon-tane mane-k'yoe-show)
International driver's license - *kokusai unten menkyosho* (koke-sie oon-tane mane-k'yoe-show) Filling, gas, service station - *gasorin sutando* (gah-so-reen stahn-doe)
Flat tire - *panku* (pahn-kuu)

I will fix the flat
Panku wo shuri shimasu
(Pahn-kuu oh shuu-ree she-mahss)

Full (tank) - *mantan* (mahn-tahn)

Shall I fill it up?
Mantan ni shimasho ka?
(Mahn-tahn nee she-mah-show kah?)

Gallon - *garon* (gah-roan)*

*In most countries of the world, gasoline is sold by the liter (reet-tah), not the gallon. One gallon equals 3.785 liters.

Gasoline - *gasorin* (gah-so-reen)
Gasoline charge - *gasorin-dai* (gah-so-reen-die)
Gasoline station - *gasorin sutando* (gah-so-reen stahn-doe)
Garage - *gareji* (gah-ray-jee)
Insurance - *hoken* (hoe-kane)

Would you like to take out insurance?
Hoken wo kaketai desu ka?
(Hoe-kane oh kah-kay-tie dess kah?)

Intersection - *kosaten* (koe-sah-tane)
Kinds/makes (of cars) - *shurui* (shuu-rue-ee)

We have several makes of cars
Su shurui no kuruma ga arimasu
(Sue shuu-rue-ee no kuu-rue-mah gah ah-ree-mahss)

Large car - *o gata* (oh gah-tah)
Leave (the car somewhere) - *norisuterimasu* (no-ree-sue-tay-ree-mahss)

Would you like to leave the car in Las Vegas?
Rasu Begasu ni kuruma wo norisutetai desu ka?
(Rahss Bay-gah-sue nee kuu-rue-mah oh no-ree-sue-tay-tie dess

kah?)

Left (direction) - *hidari* (he-dah-ree)

Turn left at the next intersection
Kono tsugi no kosaten de hidari e magatte kudasai
(Koe-no t'sue-ghee no koe-sah-tane day he-dah-ree eh mah-got-tay kuu-dah-sie)

Liter - *rittaa* (reet-tah)
Map - *chizu* (chee-zoo); *mappu* (mahp-puu)

City map - *machi no chizu* (mah-chee-no chee-zoo)
Road map - *doro no chizu* (doe-roe no chee-zoo)
Mechanic - *makenikku* (mah-kay-neek-kuu); *shuri suru hito* (shuu-ree sue-rue ssh-toe)
Medium-sized car - *chu gata* (chuu gah-tah)
Mileage - *mairu-su* (my-rue sue); *kiro-su* (kee-roe su)*

*Only Americans understand and use miles in measuring distance. Everyone else uses kilometers. All distances, rates, etc., should therefore be converted to kilometers when dealing with nonAmericans.

Su by itself means "number" or "figure." *Kiro-su* means "kilometer-age" (as in mileage).

Oil - oiru (oh-ee-rue)

Shall I check the oil?
Oiru wo shirabemasho ka?
(Oh-ee-rue oh she-rah-bay-mah-show kah?)

One-way (street) - *ippo-tsuko* (eep-poe-t'sue-koe)
Parking lot/area - *chusha jo* (chuu-shah joe)
Pedestrian crossing - *odan hodo* (oh-dahn hoe-doe)

Pedestrian overpass - *ho dokyo* (hoe-doe-k'yoe)
Rate - *ryokin* (r'yoe-keen)
Rent- *karimasu* (kah-ree-mahss)
Rental car - *renta ka* (ren-tah kah)
Small car - *kogata sha* (koe-gah-tah shah)

Which do you prefer, a small car or a large car?
Dochira ga ii desu ka, kogata sha ka ogata sha?

(Doe-chee-rah gah ee dess kah, koe-gah-tah shah kah oh-gah-tah shah?)

Speed - *sokudo* (so-kuu-doe)
Speed limit - *seigen sokudo* (say-ee-gane so-kuu-doe)
Sports car - *supotsu ka* (s'pote-sue kah)
Toll road (highway) - *kosoku doro* (koe-soe-kuu doe-roe)
Traff'lc light - *shingo* (sheen-go)
Windshield wipers - *waipa* (wie-pah)

Tipping

Tip - *chippu* (cheep-puu)*

*Japanese travelers are well aware that tipping limousine, shuttle and taxi drivers, bar and restaurant help, bellboys, porters, and certain other service personnel is commonplace outside of Japan. Many Japanese business travelers also make a practice of leaving tips for their room maids, especially if they stay in the same hotel several nights.

This contrasts dramatically with traditional tipping customs in Japan. Generally speaking, in the hospitality, food and beverage industries in Japan a service charge ranging from 10 to 20 percent is added to bills that exceed a certain amount, ostensibly in lieu of tips to individual personnel. About the only people in Japan who officially receive tips as part of their regular income are railway station and airport porters, and tourist guides. Popular hostesses in cabarets, sought-after geisha and miscellaneous others are also regularly tipped as a personal choice.

In earlier days in Japan it was common to tip service people in advance to ensure the best possible treatment.

PART 1

THE AIRLINE AND RAILWAY INDUSTRIES

Key Words & Useful Sentences

Welcome aboard! - *Irasshaimase!* (Ee-rah-shy-mah-say!)
Airline (company) - *koku kaisha* (koe-kuu kie-shah)
Airplane - *hikoki* (he-koe-kee)

Which airline (are you going on/coming in on)?
Dochira no hikoki kaisha desu ka?
(Doe-chee-rah no he-koe-kee kie-shah dess kah?)

The plane is landing now
Hikoki wa ima chakuriku shite imasu
(He-koe-kee wah ee-mah chah-kuu-ree-kuu ssh-tay ee-mahss)

Airport - *kuko* (kuu-koe)

We will soon be arriving at Kennedy Airport
Mamonaku Kenadi Kuko ni tochaku shimasu
(Mah-moe-nah-kuu Kay-nah-dee Kuu-koe nee toe-chah-kuu
she-mahss)

Air sick - *hikoki ni yoimasu* (he-koe-kee nee yoe-ee-mahss)

How are you feeling?
O'kagen wa ikaga desu ka?
(Oh-kah-gane wah ee-kah-gah dess kah?)

Are you air sick?
Hikoki ni yoimasu ka?
(He-koe-kee nee yoe-ee-mahss kah?)

Would you like to lie down?
Yoko ni naritai desu ka?
(Yoe-koe nee nah-ree-tai dess kah?)

When we land we will have an arnbulance standing by
Chakuriku itashimasu to kyukyusha ga taiki shite orimasu
Chah-kuu-ree-kuu ee-tah-she-mahss toe que-que-shah ga tie-kee
ssh-tay oh-ree-mahss)

Aisle - *tsuro* (t'suu-roe); *airu* (aye-rue)

Aisle seat - *tsuro gawa no seki* (t'suu-roe gah-wah no say-kee)

Is an aisle seat all right?
Tsuro gawa no seki wa yoroshii desu ka?
(T'sue-roe ~ah-wah no say-kee wah yoe-roe-she-ee dess kah?)

Altitude - *takasa* (tah-kah-sah); *kodo* (koe-doe)

We are flying at an altitude of 10,000 meters

Tadaima ichi man metoru jokuu wo tonde imasu
(Tah-die-mah ee-chee mahn may-toe-rue joe-kuu oh tone-day ee- mahss)

Announcement - *happyo* (hop-yoe); *annai* (ahn-nie)

May I have your attention, please!
Ladies and gentlemen, I have an announcement to make
Okyaku san ni go-annai itashimasu!
(Oh-k'yahk sahn nee go-ahn-nie ee-tah-she-mahss)

*It is customary in Japan for hotel guests, retail customers, and passengers on airplanes and other forms of transportation to be addressed as *O'kyaku San* (oh-k'yahk sahn)—which literally means "Mr. Guest," "Mrs. Guest," or "Miss Guest," whichever the case may be, as well as the plural "Guests" when addessing more than one person. O'kyaku San is also used in the sense of "Ladies and Gentlemen" when making an announcement, particularly to announce information. For example:

Ladies and gentlemen, we will be taking off in a few seconds
O'kyaku san ni, go-annai itashimasu. Mamonaku ririku itashimasu
(Oh-k'yahk sahn nee, go-ahn-nie ee-tah-she mahss. Mah-moe-nah-kuu ree-ree-kuu ee-tah-she-mahss)

Annai (ahn-nie) by itself means "information, guidance, advice" (go is an honorific). With the verb *itashimasu*, means "I am going to guide you, direct you, give you some information;" or "I am going to make an announcement/this is an announcement.

Arrive - *tsukimasu* (t'ski-mahss); *tochaku shimasu* (toe-chah-kuu she-mahss)

What time does your plane arrive?
Hikoki wa nanji ni tochaku shimasu ka?
(He-koe-kee wah nahn-jee nee toe-chah-kuu she-mahss kah?)

We will arrive in Honolulu in 30 minutes
Ato sanjip pun Honoruru ni tochaku shimasu
(Ah-toe sahn-jeep poon Hoe-no-rue-rue nee toe-chah-ku she-mahss)

Arrival - *tochaku* (toe-chah-kuu)

Arrival gate - *tochaku geito* (toe-chah-kuu gay-ee-toe)

We will be arriving at Gate 12
Juni ban geito ni tochaku shimasu
auu-nee bahn gay-ee-toe nee toe-chah-kuu she-mahss)

Arrival time - *tochaku jikan* (toe-chah-kuu jee-kahn)

Please give me (tell me) your arrival time
Tochaku jikan wo oshiete kudasai
(Toe-chah-kuu jee-kahn oh oh-she-eh-tay kuu-dah-sie)

Our arrival time will be 6:30 P.M.
Tochaku jikan wa gogo no roku ji-han desu
(Toe-chah-kuu jee-kahn wa go-go no roe-kuu-jee-hahn dess)

Because of a tail-wind, we will be earlier than scheduled
Oi-kaze desu no de yotei yori mo hayaku natte imasu
(Oh-ee-kah-zay dess no day yoe-tay-ee yoe-ree mo hah-yah-kuu
not-tay ee-mahss)

Baggage - *nimotsu* (nee-moat-sue); also *bageji* (bah-gay-jee)

Shall I take (help you) with your baggage?
O-nimotsu wo mochi itashimasho ka?
(Oh-nee-mote-sue oh moe-chee ee-tah-she-mah-show kah?)

Shall I help you (do anything)?
O'tetsudai itashimasho ka?
(Oh-tate-sue-die ee-tah-she-mah-show kah?)

Excuse me, will you please put your baggage under your seat?
*Osore irimasu ga, o'nimotsu wa zaseki no shita ni o'ire
itadakemasu ka?*
(Oh-soe-ray ee-ree-mahss ga, oh-nee-mote-sue wah zah-say-kee
no ssh-tah nee oh-ee-ray ee-tah-dah-kay-mahss kah?)

Please reclaim all of your baggage
Nimotsu wo zembu atsumete kudasai
(Nee-mote-sue oh zem-buu aht-sue-may-tay kuu-dah-sie)

Baggage claim ticket - *chikki no fuda* (cheek-kee no fuu-dah)

Please show me your claim ticket
Chikki no fuda wo misete kudasai
(Cheek-kee no fuu-dah oh me-say-tay kuu-dah-sie)

Bassinet - *bashinetto* (bah-she-net-toe)
Blanket - *mofu* (moe-fuu)

Would you like another blanket?
Mofu mo ichimai ikaga desu ka?
(Moe-fuu moe ee-chee-my ee-kah-gah dess kah?)

After we take off, I will bring you another one
Ririku itashimashitara mo ichi mae wo motte kimasu
(Ree-ree-kuu ee-tah-she-mahssh-tah-rah moe ee-chee my oh
mote-tay kee-mahss)

Board (get on the plane) - *tojo shimasu* (toe-joe she-mahss)

Your flight is boarding now
Anata no bin wa ima tojo shite imasu
(Ah-nah-tah no bean wah ee-mah toe-joe ssh-tay ee-mahss)
Boarding pass - tojo ken (toejoe ken)

Please show me your boarding pass
Tojo ken wo misete kudasai
(Toejoe ken oh me-say-tay kuu-dah-sie)

May I see your boarding pass?
Go-tojo ken wo haiken dekimasu desho ka?
(Go-toejoe ken oh hi-kane day-kee-mahss day-show kah?)

Breakfast - *asahan* (ah-sah-hahn); *choshoku* (choe-show-kuu)

This is a breakfast flight
Kore wa choshoku no bin desu
(Koe-ray wah choe-show-kuu no bean dess)

We will serve breakfast in about 30 minutes
Yaku sanjippun choshoku no jikan desu
(Yah-kuu sahnjeep-poon choe-show-kuu no jee-kahn dess)

Call button - *koru botan* (koe-rue boe-tahn)

If you want anything push the call button
Nani ka hoshikereba koru botan wo oshite kudasai
(Nah-nee kah hoe-she-kay-ray-bah koe-rue boe-tahn wo ohssh-
tay kuu-dah-sie)

Captain - *kicho* (kee-choe)

This is the captain speaking (I am the captain)
Kicho de gozaimasu
(Kee-choe day go-zie-mahss)

Carry-on baggage - *te-nimotsu* (tay-nee-moat-sue)

Please take all of your carry-on baggage (with you)
Te-nimotsu wo zembu motte itte kudasai
(Tay-nee-mote-sue oh zem-buu mote-tay eet-tay kuu-dah-sie)

Celsius - *sesshi* (say-she)*

*This refers to the temperature scale that registers the freezing point of water at 0 degrees and the boiling point at 100 degrees. The designation celsius has been official since 1948 but it is still commonly referred to as "centigrade" as well.

Centigrade temperature - *sesshi kandankei no* (say-sshe kahn-dahn-kay-ee no)

Check-in - *cheku-in* (che-kuu-een)

Please check-in by 10 o'clock
Juji made ni cheku-in shite kudasai
(Juu-jee mah-day nee cheh-kuu-een ssh-tay kuu-dah-sie)

Chopsticks - *o'hashi* (oh-hah-she)

Would you prefer chopsticks?
O'hashi no ho ga ii desu ka?
(Oh-hah-she no hoe gah eee dess kah?)

Clear (fine weather) - *kaisei de aru* (kie-say-ee day ah-rue)
Clearance - *kyoka* (k'yoe-kah)
Cleared for departure - *shuppatsu kyoka* (shupe-pot-sue k'yoe-kah)
Cleared for landing - *chakuriku kyoka* (chah-kuu-ree-kuu k'yoe-kah)

We have been cleared for landing
Chakuriku kyoka wo itashimashita
(Chah-kuu-ree-kuu k'yoe-kah oh ee-tah-she-mah-sshtah)

Cleared for take-off- *ririku kyoka* (ree-ree-kuu k'yoe-kah)

We have been cleared for take-off
Ririku kyoka wo itashimashita
(Ree-ree-kuu k'yoe-kah oh ee-tah-she-mah-sshtah)

Climate - *kiko* (kee-koe)
Climbing/ascending - *josho shimasu* (joe-show she-mahss)
Cloudy - *kumotta* (kuu-moat-tah); *kumotte imasu* (kuu-mote-tay
ee-mahss)

Chicago is cloudy with rain expected in the afternoon
Shikago wa kumotta de, gogo kara ame ga furiso desu
(She-kah-go wa kuu-mote-tah day, go-go kah-rah ah-may gah
fuu-ree-soh dess)

Coffee - kohi (koe-hee)

Would you like (a cup of) coffee?
Kohi wa ikaga desho ka?
(Koe-hee wah ee-kah-gah day-show kah?)

Would you like another cup of coffee?
Kohi no o'kawari wa ikaga desho ka?
(Koe-he no oh-kah-wah-ree wah ee-kah-gah day-show kah?)

Collect (earphones, headsets) - *atsumeru* (aht-sue-may-rue)

We will now be collecting earphones
Kore kara eahon wo o'atsume itashimasu
(Koe-ray kah-rah eh-ah-hoan oh oh-ah-t'sue-may ee-tah-she-
mahss)

Confirm Reservations - *yoyaku wo kakunin shimasu* (yoe-yah-
ku oh kah-kuu-neen she-mahss)

Please reconfirm your reservations two or three days in advance
Ni, san nichi mae ni yoyaku wo kakunin shite kudasai
(Nee, sahn nee-chee my nee yoe-yah-kuu oh kah-kuu-neen
ssh'tay kuu-dah-sie)

Have you confirmed your reservations?
Yoyaku wo kakunin shimashita ka?
(Yoe-yah-kuu oh kah-kuu-neen she-mah-ssh'tah kah?)

I will confirm your reservations
Yoyaku wo kakunin shimasu
(Yoe-yah-kuu oh kah-kuu-neen she-mahss)

Connection - *noritsugi* (no-ree-t'sue-ghee)
Connecting flight - *noritsugi bin* (noe-ree-t'sue-ghee bean)

Your connecting flight leaves from Gate 44
Anata no noritsugi bin wa yonjuyon geito kara demasu
(Ah-nah-tah no no-ree-t'sue-ghee bean wa yonejuu-yone gay-ee-toe kah-rah day-mahss)

Control tower - *kansei to* (kahn-say-ee toh)
Cruising (speed) - *suiheihiko* (suu-ee-hay-ee-he-koe)
Customs - *zeikan* (zay-ee-kahn); go through Customs - T*sukan* (t'sue-kahn)

Everyone must go through Customs
Mina san ga Tsukan wo shinakereba narimasen
(Me-nah sahn gah t'sue-kahn oh she-nah-kay-ray-bah nah-ree-mah-sin)

Customs declaration - *zeikan shinkokusho* (zay-ee-kahn sheen-koe-kuu-show)

Please fill out your customs declaration before we land
Chakuriku suru mae ni zeikan shinkokusho wo kinyu shite kudasai
(Chah-kuu-ree-kuu sue-rue my nee zay-ee-kahn sheen-koe-kuu-show oh keen-yuu ssh-tay kuu-dah-sie)

Customs duties - *kanzei* (kahn-zay-ee)
Customs off'lcer - *zeikan ri* (zay-ee-kahn ree)
Daylight saving time - *natsu jikan* (not-sue jee-kahn)

Please reset your watches to daylight saving time
Tokei wo natsu jikan ni awasete kudasai
(Toe-kay-ee oh not-sue jee-kahn nee ah-wah-say-tay kuu-dah-sie)

Departure - *shuppatsu* (shupe-pot-sue)

Your flight is scheduled to leave at 9:20 A.M.
Anata no bin wa gozen no kuji nijippun sugi ni shuppatsu no yotei desu
(Ah-nah-tah no bean wah go-zane no kuu-jee nee-jeep-poon sue-ghee nee shupe-pot-sue no yoe-tay-ee dess)

Departure gate - *tojo guchi* (toe-joe guu-chee); *tojo geito* (toe-joe gay-ee-toe)

Departure lobby- *shuppatsu machiaishitsu* (shupe-pot-sue mah-chee-aye-sheet-sue)

Departure lounge - *shuppatsu no raounji* (shupe-pot-sue no rah-oonjee); *shuppatsu machiaishitsu* (shupe-pot-sue mah-chee-aye-sheet-sue)

Departure time - *shuppatsu jikan* (shupe-pot-sue jee-kahn)

Descending - *kohka shite imasu* (koe-kah ssh-tay ee-mahss)

Dinner - *yuhan* (yuu-hahn)

What would you like for your main course? Roast beef, chicken or fish?
Shitsurei itashimasu, o'shokuji wa nani wo itashimasho ka?
Rosu bifu, chikin ka sakana?
(She-t'sue-ray-ee ee-tah-she-mahss, oh-show-kuujee wah nah-nee oh ee-tah-she-mah-show kah? Roe-sue bee-fuu, chee-keen kah, sah-kah-nah?)

We also have Japanese food
Nihon ryori mo gozaimasu
(Nee-hoan r'yoe-ree mo go-zie-mahss)

Excuse me, did you order something special?
O'sore irimasu ga, nani ka tokubetsu no chumon wo natte imasu ka?
(Oh-so-ray ee-ree-mahss gah, nah-nee kah toe-kuu-bate-sue no chuu-moan oh not-tay ee-mahss kah?)

What would you like to drink? Coffee, tea, milk or water?
Nani wo nomitai desu ka? Kohi, kocha, miruku, ka o'mizu?
(Nah-nee oh no-me-tie dess kah? Koe-hee, koe-chah, me-rue-kuu, kah oh-me-zoo?)

Drink (something to drink) - *nomimono* (no-me-moe-no)

Would you like something to drink?
Nomimono wa ikaga desho ka?
(No-me-moe-no wah ee-kah-gah day-show kah?)

Would you like something else to drink?
Hoka no nomimono wa ikaga desho ka?
(Hoe-kah no no-me-moe-no wah ee-kah-gah day-show kah?)

Shall I bring you another one (round)?
O'kawari wo mochi itashimasho ka?
(Oh-kah-wah-ree oh moe-chee ee-tah-she-mah-show kah?)

Would you like something to drink before lunch/dinner?
O'shokuji no mae ni o'nomimono wa ikaga desho ka?
(Oh-show-kuujee no my nee oh-no-me-moe-no wah ee-kah-gah
day-show kah?)

(Sorry) I kept you waiting
(Also used in the sense of "Here you are, sir/ma'am")
O'matase itashimashita
(Oh-mah-tah-say ee-tah-she-mahssh-tah)

Duty free - *mu zei* (muu zay-ee)
Duty free merchandise - *mu zei hin* (muu zay-ee heen)

Are you interested in (buying) some duty-free items?
Muzei hin no yo wa gozaimasu ka?
(Muu-zay-ee heen no yoh wah go-zie-mahss kah?)

All together it comes to $88
Zembu de hachijuhachi doru de gozaimasu
(Zem-buu day hah-chee-juu-hah-chee doe-rue day go-zie-mahss

Do you have any small bills (currency)?
Shogaku shihei ga gozaimasu ka?
(Show-gah-kuu she-hay-ee gah go-zie-mahss kah?)

Here is your change
O'tsuri de gozaimasu
(Oh-t'sue-ree day go-zie-mahss)

Please count/verify your change
O'tsuri wo o'tashikame kudasai
(Oh-t'sue-ree oh oh'tah-she-kah-may kuu-dah-sie)

I'm sorry, we do not carry/stock that
Moshiwake gozaimasen, sore wa tosai shite orimasen
(Moe-she-wah-kay go-zie-mah-sin, soe-ray wah toe-sie ssh-tay
oh-ree-mah-sin)

I'm very sorry, we've sold out of that
Taihen moshiwake gozaimasen, sore wo urikirete shimaimashita
(Tie-hane moe-she-wah-kay go-zie-mah-sin, soe-ray oh uu-ree-kee-ray-tay she-my-mah-sshtah)

Ears - *mimi* (me-me)

Are your ears blocked (hurting)?
Mimi ga tsumatte imasu ka?
(Me-me gah t'sue-mot-tay ee-mahss kah?)

Please swallow (to clear your ears)
Tsuba wo nomikonde kudasai
(T'sue-bah oh no-me-kone-day kuu-dah-sie)

Please close your mouth, hold your nose and blow
Kuchi wo shimete, hana wo tsumande, kuki wo fuite kudasai
(Kuu-chee oh she-may-tay, hah-nah oh t'sue-mahn-day, kuu-kee oh fuu-ee-tay kuu-dah-sie

How are your ears now?
Ima mimi no choshi ga ikaga desu ka?
(Ee-mah me-me no choe-she gah ee-kah-gah dess kah?)

Economy Class - *ekonomi kurasu* (eh-koe-no-me kuu-rah-sue)
Emergency - *hijoji* (he-joe-jee)
Emergency door - *hijo no doa* (he-joe no doe-ah)
Emergency exit - *hijo no guchi* (he-joe no guu-chee)
Equator - *sekido* (say-kee-doh)
Fahrenheit - *kashi kandankei no* (kah-she kahn-dahn-kay-ee no)
Film (movie) - *eiga* (eh-ee-gah)

The movie will start after lunch is finished
Hiruhan wo sunde kara eiga ga hajimarimasu
(He-rue-han oh soon-day kah-rah eh-ee-gah gah hah-jee-mah-ree-mahss)

Final approach - *saishu chakuriku taisei* (sie-shuu cha-kuu-ree-kuu tie-say-ee)
Flight - *bin* (bean); *furaito* (fuu-rye-toe)

Flight attendant - *suchuwadesu* (sue-chuu-wah-dess)

Can I get you/bring you anything else?

Hoka ni nani ka omochi itashimasho ka?
Hoe-kah nee nah-nee kah oh-moe-chee ee-tah-she-mah-show
kah?)

If you need/want anything else, please let me know
*Nani ka gozaimashitara, dozo go-enryonaku o-moshitsuke
kudasaimase*
(Nah-nee kah go-zie-mahssh-tah-rah, doe-zoe go-inn-r'yoe-nah-
kuu oh-moe-she-t'skay
kuu-dah-sie-mah-say)

Flight number - *bin no bango* (bean-no bahn-go); *furaito namba*
(fuu-rye-toe nahm-bah)

What is your flight number?
Furaito namba wa nan desu ka?
Fuu-rye-toe nahm-bah wah nahn dess kah?)

Flight time - *hiko jikan* (he-koe jee-kahn)

The flight time from San Francisco to Tokyo is about 10 hours
*San Furanshisuko kara Tokyo made no hiko jikan wa daitai juji
kan desu*
(Sahn Fuu-rahn-shees-koe kah-rah Toe-k'yoe mah-day no hee-
koe jee-kahn wah die-tie juu-jee kahn dess)

Flotation pillow - *fudo zaseki kushon* (fuu-doe zah-say-kee kuu-
shoan)

First-Class - *fasuto kurasu* (fahss-toe kuu-rah-sue)

First-class passengers may board any time
Fasuto kurasu no okyaku san ga nanji de mo notte mo ii desu
(Fahss-toe kuu-rah-sue no oh'k'yah-kuu sahn gah nahn-jee day
moe note-tay moe ee dess)

Fog - *kiri* (kee-ree); foggy - *kiri-bukai* (kee-ree-buu-kie)

It is foggy
Kiri ga fukai desu
(Kee-ree gah fuu-kie dess)

Gate - *tojo-guchi* (toe-joe guu-chee); *geito* (gay-ee-toe)
Go through Customs - *tsukan* (t'sue-kahn)

In Los Angeles you must go through Customs

Rosu Anjiresu de Tsukan wo shinakereba narimasen
(Roass Ahn-jee-ray-sue day t'sue-kahn oh she-nah-kay-ray-bah
nah-ree-mah-sin)

Handicapped person(s) - *handikyappu no kata* (hahn-dee-k'yahp-puu no kah-tah)

Hang up coat - *koto wo kakemasu* (koe-toe oh kah-kay-mahss)
Haze - *moya* (moe-yah); *kasunda* (kah-soon-dah)
Hazy weather - *kasunda tenki* (kah-soon-dah tane-kee)
Ice - *kori* (koe-ree); *aisu* (aye-sue)

Shall I bring you some ice?
Aisu wo motte kimasho ka?
(Aye-sue oh mote-tay kee-mah-show kah?)

Individually (one-by-one) - *hitori hitori ni* (ssh-toe-ree ssh-toe-ree nee)

Please enter one-by-one
Hitori hitori ni haitte kudasai
(Ssh-toe-ree ssh-toe-ree nee hite-tay kuu-dah-sie)

Inflight - *kinai* (kee-nie)
Inflight service - *kinai sabisu* (kee-nie sah-bee-sue)

Did you call (me)?
Oyobi desho ka?
(Oh-yoe-bee day-show kah?)

What can I do for you?
Nani wo itashimasho ka?
(Nah-nee oh ee-tah-she-mah-show kah?)

Would you like to recline your seat?
Zaseki no se wo taoshi ni naritai desu ka?
(Zah-say-kee no say oh tah-oh-she nee nah-ree-tie dess kah?)

Shall I hang up/put away/check your coat?
Koto wo o'atsukari itashimasho ka?
(Koe-toe oh oh-aht-sue-kah-ree ee-tah-she-mah-show kah?)

If you need anything, please let me know
Nani ka go yo ga gozaimashitara o'shirase kudasai
(Nah-nee kah go yoh gah go-zie-mahss-tah-rah oh-she-rah-say
kuu-dah-sie)

Information counter - *annai kaunta* (ahn-nie kah-oon-tah)

For more details please ask at the arrival lobby information counter
Kuwashii koto wa tochaku robi no annai kaunta de o'tazune kudasai
(Kuu-wah-she-ee koe-toe wah toe-chah-kuu roe-bee no ahn-nie kah-oon-tah day oh-tah-zoo-nay kuu-dah-sie)

International Date Line - *Kokusai Hizuke Henko Sen* (koke-sie he-zoo-kay hane-koe sin)

We have just now crossed the International Date Line
Tadaima Kokusai Hizuke Henko Sen wo koemashita
(Tah-die-mah Koke-sie He-zoo-kay Hane-koe Sin oh koe-eh-mah-sshtah)

Jet-lag (same as time difference) - *jissa* (jees-sah)

Are you suffering from jet-lag?
Jissa boke desu ka?
(jees-sah boh-kay dess kah?)

Land, landing - *chakuriku* (chah-kuu-ree-kuu)

We will be landing momentarily
Mamonaku chakuriku itashimasu
(Mah-moe-nah-kuu chah-kuu-ree-kuu ee-tah-she-mahss)

Ladies and gentlemen, we will be landing at Tokyo International Airport in 30 minutes
O'kyaku san ni, go-annai itashimasu. Tadaima kara yoso sanjip pun de Shin Tokyo Kokusai Kuko ni chakuriku itashimasu
(Oh'k-yahk sahn nee, go-ahn-nie ee-tah-she-mahss. Tah-die-mah kah-rah yoe-so sahn-jeep poon day Sheen Toe-k'yoe Koke-sie Kuu-koe nee chah-kuu-ree-kuu ee-tah-she-mahss)

Please make sure your seat belt is fastened
O'zaseki no beruto wo o'shime ka do ka, mo ichido o'tashikame kudasai
(Oh-zah-say-kee no bay-rue-toe oh oh-she-may kah doe kah, moe ee-chee-doe oh-tah-she-kah-may kuu-dah-sie)

Life preserver - *kyumei bukuro* (que-may-ee buu-kuu-roe)
Lightning - *kaminari* (kah-me-nah-ree)

Local time - *genchi jikan* (gane-chee jee-kahn)

Local time is now 3 p.m.
Genchi jikan wa ima sanji desu
(Gane-chee jee-kahn wah ee-mah sahn-jee dess)

Lunch - *hiruhan* (he-rue-hahn); *ranchi* (rahn-chee)
Magazine - *zasshi* (zahs-she)

Would you like a magazine?
Zasshi wa ikaga desu ka?
(Zahs-she wah ee-kah-gah dess kah?)

We have several Japanese-language magazines
Su Nihongo no zasshi ga arimasu
(Sue Nee-hoan-go no zahs-she gah ah-ree-mahss)

Navigator - *kokaicho* (koe-kie-choe)
Newspaper - *shimbun* (sheem-boon)

We also have Japanese language newspapers
Nihongo no shimbun mo arimasu
(Nee-hoan-go no sheem-boon moe ah-ree-mahss)

Excuse me. Have you finished with that newspaper?
Shitsurei itashimasu. Sono shimbun wo o'sumi desho ka?
(Sheet-sue-ray-ee ee-tah-she-mahss. Soe-no sheem-boon oh oh-sue-me day-show kah?)

Now boarding - *tojo chu* (toe-joe chuu)

Your flight is boarding now
Anato no bin wa ima tojo chu desu
(Ah-nah-tah no bean wa ee-mah toejoe chuu dess)

Peninsula - *hanto* (hahn-toe)
Pilot - *pairetto* (pie-rate-toe); *sojushi* (soe-juu-she)
Purser - *paasa* (pah-sah)
One-way - *kata-michi* (kah-tah-me-chee)
One-way ticket - *kata-michi no ken* (kah-tah-me-chee no ken)
Open seating - *jiyu seki* (jee-yuu say-kee)

This flight will be open seating
Kono bin wa jiyu seki desu
(Koe-no bean wah jee-yuu say-kee dess)

Overhead bin (compartment) - *zujo shunoko* (zoo-joe shuu-no-koe)

Oxygen - *sansui* (sahn-suu-ee)

Oxygen mask - *sansui no masuku* (sahn-suu-ee no mahss-kuu)

Passenger; guest - *tojosha* (toejoe-shah); *o'kyaku san* (oh-k'yahk sahn)

Physical disability - *shintai shogai* (sheen-tie show-guy)

Rain - *ame* (ah-may); *ame ga furimasu* (ah-may gah fuu-ree-mahss)

It is raining in Paris
Pari de ame ga futte imasu
(Pah-ree day ah-may gah fute-tay ee-mahss)

It appears that it will rain tomorrow
Ashita ame ga furi so desu
(Ah-ssh-tah ah-may gah fuu-ree soh dess)

The rain will stop by tonight
Komban made ame ga yamemasu
(Kome-bahn mah-day ah-may gah yah-may-mahss)

Reservations - *yoyaku* (yoe-yah-kuu)

Reconfirm reservations - *yoyaku wo kakunin shimasu* (yoe-yah-kuu oh kah-kuu-neen she-mahss)

Don't forget to reconfirm your reservations
Yoyaku wo kakunin suru no wa wasurenai de kudasai
(Yoe-yah-kuu oh kah-kuu-neen sue-rue no wah wah-sue-ray-nie day kuu-dah-sie)

Roundtrip - *ofuku* (oh-fuu-kuu) Roundtrip ticket - *ofuku ken* (oh-fuu-kuu ken)

Do you have a round-trip ticket?
Ofuku ken wo motte imasu ka?
(Oh-fuu-kuu ken oh mote-tay ee-mahss kah?)

Runway - *kassoro* (kahss-soe-roh)

Sand storm - *suna kaze* (sue-nah kah-zay)

Scotch whiskey - *sukochi uisuki* (suu-koe-chee we-ski)

Schedule, plan - *yotei* (yoe-tay-ee)

We are scheduled to arrive at 3 P.M.
Gogo no sanji ni tochaku suru yotei desu
(Go-go no sahnjee nee toe-chah-kuu sue-rue yoe-tay-ee dess)

Seat - *seki* (say-kee); *shiito* (shee-toe)

Please take your seats
Dozo, okake kudasaimase
(Doe-zoe, oh-kah-kay kuu-da-sie-mah-say)

*Adding *mase* to *kudasai* makes it much more polite.

Seat assignment (reservation) - *seki no yoyaku* (say-kee no yoe-yah-kuu)
Seat belt - *shiito beruto* (shee-toe bay-rue-toe); *zaseki beruto* (zah-say-kee bay-rue-toe)

Please fasten your seat belts
O'zaseki beruto wo o'shime kudasai
(Oh-zah-say-kee bay-rue-toe oh oh-she-may kuu-dah-sie)

Will you please fasten your seat belt?*
Osoreirimasu ga, zaseki no beruto wo oshime itadakemasu desho ka?
(Oh-soe-ray-ee-ree-mahss gah, zah-say-kee no bay-rue-toe oh oh-she-may ee-tah-dah-kay-mahss day-show kah?)

*Very polite; appropriate when speaking directly to an individual.

Seat next to the window - *mado giwa no seki* (mah-doe ghee-wah no say-kee)

Seat number - *seki no namba* (say-kee no nahm-bah); shiito namba (shee-toe nahm-bah)

What is your seat number?
Shiito namba wa nan de gozaimasu ka?
(Shee-toe nahm-bah wah nahn day go-zie-mahss kah?)

Excuse me, this is not your seat
Sumimasen ga, kore wa anata no seki dewa arimasen
(Sue-me-mah-sin gah, koe-ray wah ah-nah-tah no say-kee day-wah ah-ree-mah-sin)

It is not open seating
Jiyu seki de wa arimasen
(Jee-yuu say-kee day wah ah-ree-mah-sin)

Serve (meals) - *dashimasu* (dah-she-mahss)

We will serve lunch in about thirty minutes
Yaku sanjippun de ranchi wo dashimasu
(Yah-kuu sahn-jeep-poon day rahn-chee oh dah-she-mahss)

Sick - *byoki* (b'yoe-kee)

Are you sick?
Byoki desu ka?
(B'yoe-kee dess kah?)

Do you have an upset stomach?
I no guai ga warui no desu ka?
(Ee no guu-wie gah wah-rue-ee no dess kah?)

Do you have an allergy?
Arerugi wa gozaimasu ka?
(Ah-ray-rue-ghee wah go-zie-mahss kah?)

Single line - ichi retsu (ee-chee ray-t'sue)

Please form a single line
Ichi retsu ni narande kudasai
(Ee-chee ray-t'sue nee nah-rahn-day kuu-dah-sie)

Snack - *sunakku* (sue-nock-kuu)

We will serve a snack before arriving
Tochaku suru mae ni sunakku wo dashimasu
(Toe-chah-kuu sue-rue my nee sue-nock-kuu oh dah-she-mahss)

Would you like a snack?
Sunakku wa ikaga desho ka?
(Sue-nahk-kuu wah ee-kah-gah day-show kah?)

Snow - *yuki* (yuu-kee); to snow - *yuki ga furimasu* (yuu-kee gah fuu-ree-mahss)
Snowdrift - *yuki no fukidamari* (yuu-kee no fuu-kee-dah-mah-ree)
Snowfall - *yukifuri* (yuu-kee-fuu-ree)
Snowslide - *yukinadare* (yuu-kee-nah-dah-ray)
Snowstorm - *fubuki* (fuu-buu-kee)

We will depart after the snow stops

Yuki ga yande kara shuppatsu shimasu
(Yuu-kee gah yahn-day kah-rah shupe-pot-sue she-mahss)

After it stops snowing, it will get very cold
Yuki ga yande kara taihen samuku ni narimasu
(Yuu-kee gah yahn-day kah-rah tie-hane sah-muu-kuu nee nah-ree-mahss)

Storm - *arashi* (ah-rah-she)
Stormy weather - *areta tenko* (ah-ray-tah tane-koe)
Tail wind - *oi-kaze* (oh-ee-kah-zay)

We are expecting a strong tail wind
Tsuyoi oi-kaze ga aru to omoimasu
(T'sue-yoe-ee oh-ee-kah-zay gah ah-rue toe oh-moy-mahss)

Take off (leave the ground) - *ririku* (ree-ree-kuu)

We will be taking off momentarily
Mamonaku ririku itashimasu
(Mah-moe-nah-kuu ree-ree-kuu ee-tah-she-mahss)

Taxiing - *kasso* (kahss-soh)
Temperature (of the air) - *ondo* (own-doe)

The temperature in New York is 20 degrees Celsius
Nu Yoku no ondo wa sesshi niju do desu
(Nuu Yoe-kuu no own-doe wah say-she nee-juu doe dess)

Temperature (of the body) - *taion* (tie-own)

I will take your temperature
Taion wo hakarimasu
(Tie-own oh hah-kah-ree-mahss)

Your temperature is a little high
Taion ga sukoshi takai desu
(Tie-own gah sue-koe-she tah-kie dess)

Ticket - *ken* (ken); *josha-ken* (joe-shah-ken); *kippu* (keep-puu)

Please show me your ticket
Kippu wo misete kudasai
(Keep-puu oh me-say-tay kuu-dah-sie)

Time difference - *jissa* (jee-sah)

In winter, the time difference between Los Angeles and Tokyo
is seven hours.
In summer it is eight hours
Fuyu ni Rosu Anjiresu to Tokyo no jissa wa shichiji kan desu.
Natsu ni hachiji kan desu
(Fuu-yuu nee Roass Ahnjee-ray-sue toe Toe-k'yoe no jees-sah
wah she-chee-jee kahn dess.
Not-sue nee hah-chee-jee kahn dess)

Toilet - *toire* (toe-ee-ray)
Tray- *obon* (oh-bone)
VIP - *Bi-Ai-Pi* (Bee-Aye-Pee)
VIP lounge - *Bi-Ai-Pi raunji* (Bee-Aye-Pee Rounjee)

I will escort you to the VIP lounge
Bi-Ai-Pi raunji ni annai shimasu
(Bee-Aye-Pee rounjee nee ahn-nie she-mahss)

Visa - *bisa* (bee-sah)

This visa has expired
Kono bisa wa kiremashita
(Koe-no bee-sah wah kee-ray-mah-shhtah)

You must apply for a new visa
Atarashii bisa wo moshikoma-nakereba naranai desu
(Ah-tah-rah-she-ee bee-sah oh moe-she-koe-mah-nah-kay-ray-
bah nah-rah-nie dess)

Weather - *tenki* (tane-kee)
Weather report - *tenki yoho* (tane-kee yoe-hoe)

Clear - *kaisei* (kie-say-ee)
Cloudy - *kumori* (kuu-moe-ree)

Dust storm - *hokori kaze* (hoe-koe-ree kah-zay)
Fair - *hare* (hah-ray)
Foggy - *kiri-bukai* (kee-ree-buu-kie)
Hazy - *moya no kakatta* (moe-yah no kah-kaht-tah)
High humidity - *ta shitsu* (tah sheet-sue)
Low humidity - *tei shitsu* (tay-ee sheet-sue)
Rainy - ame no (ah-may no)
Sandstorm - *sunakaze* (suu-nah-kah-zay)
Snowy - *yuki no* (yuu-kee no)
Thunderstorm - *raiu* (rye-uu)

Tornado - *tatsumaki* (tah-t'sue-mah-kee)
Typhoon - *taifu* (tie-fuu)
Windstorm - *bofu* (boe-fuu)

Whiskey - *uisuki* (we-ski)
Wind - *kaze* (kah-zay)
Windy - *kaze ga fukimasu* (kah-zay ga fukimasu)

The wind is blowing today
Kyo wa kaze ga fuite imasu
K'yoe wah kah-zay gah fuu-ee-tay ee-mahss)

There is a very strong wind on top of the mountain
Yama no chojo ni taihen tsuyoi kaze ga arimasu
(Yah-mah no choe-joe nee tie-hane t'sue-yoe-ee kah-zay gah ah-ree-mahss)

Window - *mado* (mah-doe)

Do you want to sit next to the window?
Mado no soba ni suwaritai desu ka?
(Mah-doe no so-bah nee suu-wah-ree-tie dess kah?)

Window seat - *madogawa zaseki* (mah-doe-gah-wah zah-say-kee)

Will a window seat be all right?
Madogawa zaseki ga yoroshii desho ka?
(Mah-doe-gah-wah zah-say-kee gah yoe-roe-she-ee day-show kah?)

Wind turbulence - *kaze de yureru* (kah-zay day yuu-ray-rue);
rankiryu (rahn-kee-r'yuu)

We are experiencing a little turbulence, so please fasten your seat belts
Kaze de yuremasu no de o'zaseki no beruto wo o'shime kudasaimase
(Kah-zay de yuu-ray-mahss no day oh'zah-say-kee no bay-rue-toe oh oh-she-may kuu-dah-sie-mah-say)

Wine - *budoshu* (buu-doe-shuu); *wainu* (wie-nuu)

Would you like some wine?
Wainu wa ikaga desu ka?
(Wie-nuu wah ee-kah-gah dess kah?)

Inflight Shopping

Inflight sales - *kinai hambai* (kee-nie hahm-by)
Tax-free - *men-zei* (mane-zay-ee); tax-free merchandise - *men-zei hin* (mane-zay-ee heen)

Would you like (to buy) some tax-free items?
Men-zei hin wa ikaga desu ka?
(Mane-zay-ee heen wah ee-kah-gah dess kah?)

Shopping guide - *shopingu gaido* (show-peen-guu guy-doe)

Here is a copy of the (tax-free) shopping guide
Shopingu gaido wo dozo
(Show-peen-guu guy-doe oh doe-zoe)

It lists all of the items that we have for sale
Kisai sarete iru mono ga zembu dete imasu
(Kee-sie sah-ray-tay ee-rue moe-no gah zem-buu day-tay ee-mahss)

Pearls - *shinju* (sheen-juu)
Perfume - *kosui* (koe-sue-ee)
Anything else - *hoka ni nani ka* (hoe-kah nee nah-nee kah)

Would you like anthing else?
Hoka ni nani ka ikaga desho ka?
(Hoe-kah nee nah-nee kah ee-kah-gah day-show ka?)

Cabin Crew Announcements

Good morning, ladies and gentlemen
Mina san, ohayo gozaimasu
(Mee-nah sahn, oh-hah-yoe go-zie-mahss)

Good afternoon/evening, ladies and gentlemen
Gotojo no mina san
(Go-toe-joe no mee-nah sahn)

We are sorry for the delay
Mina san, omatase itashimashita
(Mee-nah sahn, oh-mah-tah-say ee-tah-she-mah-sshtah)

Thank you for flying _____ Airlines today

Honjitsu wa _____ *wo go-riyo kudasaimashite, arigato gozaimasu*
(Hoan-jeet-sue wah _____ oh go-ree-yoe kuu-dah-sie-mahsshtay, ah-ree-gah-toe go-zai-mahss)

This is flight number 10 bound for Tokyo
Kono furaito wa Tokyo yuki no ju bin desu
(Koe-no fuu-rye-toe wah Tokyo yuu-kee no juu bean dess)

Please make sure your carry-on luggage is stored beneath the seat in front of you
Tenimotsu wo zaseki no shita ni oshimai kudasai
(Tay-nee-moat-sue oh zah-say-kee no sshtah nee oh-she-my kuu-dah-sie)

Please return your seat-backs to their upright position
Shiito no sei wo moto no ichi ni omodoshi kudasai
(Shee-toe no say-ee oh moe-toe no ee-chee nee oh-moe-doe-she kuu-dah-sie)

Please lock your tray in its up position
Teburu wo moto no ichi ni omodoshi kudasai
(Tay-buu-rue oh moe-toe no ee-chee nee oh-moe-doe-she kuu-dah-sie)

Please use caution when stowing and removing items from the overhead bins to prevent things from falling out
Zujo shunoko wo otsukai ni nareru toki wa o'nimotsu ga ue kara ochinai yo jubun o'kiwotsukete kudasai
(Zoo-joe shuu-no-koe oh oh-t'sue-kie nee nah-ray-rue toe-kee wa ohnee-moat-sue gah way kah-rah oh-chee-nie yoe juu-boon oh-kee-oatskay-tay kuu-dah-sie)

Please assume the brace position
Kinkyuji no shisei wo shite kudasai
(Keen-que-jee no she-say-ee oh sshtay kuu-dah-sie)

Please do not smoke in the No Smoking sections of the cabins or in the lavatories, or when the No Smoking sign is on. Smoking is also prohibited when oxygen masks are in use.
Kaku kyabin no kin'in basho de wa, joji senmenjo ni te, kin'in no sain ga tsuita toki mo, tobako wo osui ni naranai de kudasai. Sansu masuku no shiyochu wa kin'in desu.
(Kah-kuu k'yah-bean no keen-een bah-show day wah, joe-jee senmane-joe nee tay, keen-een no sigh een gah t'sue-ee-tah toe-kee moe, toe-bah-koe oh oh-sue-ee nee nah-rah-nie day kuu-

dah-sie. Sahn-sue mah-sue-kuu no she-yoe-chuu wah keen-een
dess)

Please fasten your seat belts and observe the No Smoking sign
until it is turned off
O'zaseki no beruto wo shime; kin'en no sain ga kieru made
tabako wa goenryo kudasai
(Oh-zah-say-kee no bay-rue-toe oh she-may; keen-inn no sign
gah keeeh-rue mah-day tah-bah-koe wa go-inn-r'yoe kuu-dah-
sie)

This is a non-smoking flight
Kore wa kin-en no bin desu
(Koe-ray wah keen-een no bean dess)

The weather enroute will be mostly clear
Tochu no tenko wa daitai hare
(Toe-chuu no tane-koe wa die-tie hah-ray)

We are expecting some air turbulence during the flight
Tochu, kanrei zensen no eikyo de yureru so desu ga
(Toe-chuu, kahn-ray-ee zen-sen no eh-ee-k'yoe day yuu-ray-rue
so dess gah)

Ladies and gentlemen, the seat-belt sign has been turned off
Mina san, tadaima, beruto no sain ga kiemashita
(Me-nah sahn, tah-die-mah, bay-rue-toe no sign gah kee-eh-
mah-ssh tah)

We will be serving drinks and a light snack shortly
Mamonaku nomimono to karui shokuji wo sabisu itashimasu
(Mah-moe-nah-kuu no-me-moe-no to kah-rue-ee show-kuu-jee
oh sahbee-sue ee-tah-she-mahss)

During the flight if there is anything we can do for you, please
push your call button
Hiko chu, goyo no sai wa, koru botan wo osshite kudasai
(He-koe chuu, go-yoe sie wah, koe-rue boe-tahn oh oh-ssh-tay
kuudah-sie)

Here are the Japanese versions of other common
announcements made by flight crewmembers before and after
take-off:

Carry-on baggage must be stowed under a seat, in an endosed
overhead bin, or in a closet during take-off and landing.

*Kinai mochi komi no tenimotsu wa richakuriku no sai, kanarazu
mae no zaseki no shita, zujo no tenimotsu ire, mata wa
shunodana ni o'ire kudasai.*
(Kee-nie moe-chee koe-me no tay-nee-moat-sue wa ree-chah-
kuu-reekuu no sie, kah-nah-rah-zoo my no zah-say-kee no ssh-
tah, zoojoe no tay-nee-moat-sue ee-ray, mah-tah wah shuu-no-
dah-nah nee oh'ee-ray kuu-dah-sie)

Televisions, AM/FM radios, portable cellular telephones,
remote-control toys, and similar electronic devices must not be
used on board because they may interfere with communications.
*Kinai de wa kokuki no koshin ya koko no tame no denta bogai
ni naru terebi, rajio, keitai denwa, rajio kantororu no omocha,
mata sore ni duiji shita isai no denki seihin wo go sho ni
naranai yo onegai itashimasu.*
(Kee-nai day wah koe-kuu-kee no koe-sheen yah, koe-koe no
tah-may no dane-tah boe-guy nee nah-rue tay-ray-bee, rah-jee-
oh, kay-ee-tie dane-wah, rahjee-oh kahn-toe-roe-rue no oh-moe-
chah, mah-tah soeray nee duu-ee-jee sshtah ee-sie no dane-kee
say-ee-heen oh go show nee nah-rah-nie yoe oh-nay-guy ee-tah-
she-mahss)

All passengers (or one per family) are required to complete
Customs Declaration forms prior to arrival in the U.S. The
forms will be distributed in flight. They should include all
personal data in English and be filled out in capital letters.
Please make sure you sign your name on the backside of the
form.
*Beikoku no mokutekichi ni tochaku suru mae ni o'kyaku sama
no sen iin (mata wa kazoku de ichimae) ni wa, Zeikan Shinkoku
yoshie no go-kinyu wo onegaishite orimasu. Shinkoku yoshi wa
tochaku mae ni kinai ni te okobori itashimasu. Yoshi ni wa Eigo
no O-moji de kojinteki na joho jiko wo o'kinyu kudasai. Sore to,
yoshi no rimen ni go-jishin no go-shomei wo owasure ni
naranai yo onegai itashimasu.*
(Bay-ee-koe-kuu no moe-kuu-tay-kee-chee nee toe-chah-kuu
sue-rue my nee oh'k'yah-kuu sah-mah no sen ee-een (mah-tah
wah kah-zoekuu day ee-chee-my) nee wah, Zay-ee-kahn Sheen-
koe-kuu yoe-she-eh no go-keen-yuu oh oh-nay-guy sshtay oh-
ree-mahss. Sheen-koe-kuu yoe-she wah toe-chah-kuu my nee
kee-nie nee tay oh-koe-boe-ree eetah-she-mahss. Yoe-she nee
wah Eh-ee-go no Oh-moe-jee day koejeen-tay-kee nah joe-hoe
jee-koe oh oh-keen-yuu kuu-dah-sie. Soe-ray
toe, yoe-shee no ree-mane ne go-jee-sheen no go-show-may-ee
oh ohwah-sue-ray nee nah-rah-nie yoh oh-nay-guy ee-tah-she-
mahss.)

Prior to arrival in the U.S. all foreign nationals (except Canadian citizens and those who are permanent residents of the U.S.) are required to complete an I-94 Form. One form is required for each family member. Passengers should complete all personal and travel-related information requested on the front side of the form. Please do not write on the back side of the form. All information should be written in English, in capital letters. You are required to keep this form until your departure from the U.S.

Beikoku ni nyukoku sareru gaikokujin no kata (Kanada shimin, Beikoku ejuken hojisho nozoku) wa shunyukoku kado ("I" kyuju-yon no shoshiki) no go-kinyu ga hitsuyo to narimasu. Go-kazoku de nyukoku sareru bai de mo, kaku kojin ni taishite ichimae zutsu wo go-kinyu onegai shite orimasu. Okyaku sama no pasonaru deta oyobi ryoko nai yo to wo yoshi hyomen ni Eigo no o-moji de go-kinyu kudasai Rimen ni wa nani mo go-kinyu nasaranai yo onegai itashimasu. Kono kaado wa Beikoku wo shukoku wo sareru toki made, keitai koto ga gimu tsukerarete orimasu.

(Bay-ee-koe-kuu nee n'yuu-koe-kuu sah-ray-rue guy-koe-kuu-jeen no kah-tah (Kah-nah-dah she-meen, Bay-ee-koe-kuu eh juu-ken hoe-jee-show no-zoe-kuu) wah shuu-n'yuu-koe-kuu kah-doe [Eye-quejuu-yon no show-shee-kee] no go-keen-yuu ga heet-sue-yoe to nah-ree-mahss. Go-kah-zoe-kuu day n'yuu-koe-kuu sah-ray-rue by day moe, kah-kuu koejeen nee tie-sshtay ee-chee-my zoot-sue oh go-keen-yuu oh-nay-guy sshtay oh-ree-mahss. Oh-k'yahk sah-mah no pah-so-nah-rue day-tah oh-yoe-bee r'yoe-koe nie yoe toe oh yoe-she h'yoe-mane nee Eh-ee-go no oh-moejee day go-keen-yuu kuu-dah-sie. Ree-mane nee wah nahnee moe go-keen-yuu nah-sah-rah-nie yoh oh-nay-guy ee-tah-sheemahss. Koe-no kaah-doe wah Bay-ee-koe-kuu oh shuu-koe-kuu wo sah-ray-rue toe-kee mah-day, kay-ee-tie koe-toe ga ghee-muu t'sue-kayrah-ray-tay oh-ree-mahss.)

Smoking is prohibited on all flights within the Continental U.S., also on flights serving Alaska, Canada, Bermuda, San Juan and Cancun, as well as on flights between the mainland U.S. and Hawaii, and within Hawaii and Australia. On flights where smoking is allowed, smoking is prohibited in the lavatories, aisles, and while the No Smoking sign is illuminated. When smoking is permitted, only cigarette smoking is allowed in the smoking sections.

Beikoku hondo nai no subete, Beikoku hondo to Arasuka kan, Kanada kan, Berumuda kan, San Wan kan, Cancun kan, Hawaii kan, oyobi Hawaii to Osutoraria no kaku kuko kan no bin de

wa, joji kin'in to natte orimasu. Sono hoka no bin de mo, kin'in sain ga dento sarete iru aida, oyobi otearai, tsuro de no tabako wa kakaku okotowari shimasu. Kitsuen ga yurusareru bai demo kitsuen sekushon de no kamimaki tabako no kitsuen dake ni kagirarete orimasu no de ashikarazu go ryosho kudasai.
(Bay-ee-koe-kuu hoan-doe nie no sue-bay-tay, Bay-ee-koe-kuu hoandoe toe Ah-rahss-kah kahn, Kah-nah-dah kahn, Bay-rue-muu-dah kahn, Sahn Wahn kahn, Kahn-koon kahn, Hah-wah-ee kahn, oh-yoebee Hah-wah-ee toe Oh-sue-toe-rah-ree-ah no kah-kuu kuu-koe kahn no bean day way, joe-jee keen-een toe not-tay oh-ree-mahss. So-no hoe-kah no bean day moe, keen-een sah-een gah dane-toe sah-ray-tay ee-rue aye-dah, oh-yoe-bee oh-tay-ah-rye, t'sue-row day no tah-bah-koe wa kah-kah-kuu oh-koe-toe-wah-ree she-mahss. Keet-sue-en yuu-ruesah-ray-rue by day-moe, keet-sue-inn seh-kuu-shone day no kah-memah-kee tah-bah-koe no keet-sue-inn dah-kay nee kah-ghee-rah-ray-tay oh-ree-mahss no day ah-she-kah-rah-zoo go r'yoe-show kuu-dah-sie)

Train Talk

Train - *densha* (dane-shah)*; *ressha* (ray-sshah)

*During the streetcar era in Japan *densha* generally referred to streetcars rather than trains (it literally means "electric vehicle"). Now it is more or less interchangeable with *ressha*.

This is your train
Kore wa anata no densha desu
(Koe-ray wah ah-nah-tah no dane-shah dess)

Arrive - *tsukimasu* (t'ski-mahss)

The train from Chicago arrives at 2 P.M.
Shikago kara no ressha wa gogo no niji ni tsukimasu
(She-kah-go kah-rah no rays-shah wah go-go no nee-jee nee t'ski-mahss)

The train for New York leaves at 2:20 P.M.
Nyu Yoku yuki no ressha wa niji nijippun tsugi ni demasu
(N'yuu yoe-kuu yuu-kee no ray-sshah wa nee-jee nee-jeep-poon t'sue-ghee nee day-mahss)

Arrival platform - *tochaku homu* (toe-chah-kuu hoe-muu)

The train will arrive at platform number seven
Ressha wa nana ban homu ni tochaku shimasu
(Rays-shah wah nah-nah bahn hoe-muu nee toe-chah-kuu she-mahss)

Arriving train - *kondo no densha* (kone-doe no dane-shah)

The train coming now does not stop here
Kondo no densha wa koko de tomarimasen
(Koan-doe no dane-shah wa koe-koe day toe-mah-ree-mah-sin)

Book of tickets - *kaisu ken* (kie-sue ken)
Cancel - *kyanseru* (k'yahn-say-rue)

Shall I cancel your reservations?
Yoyaku wo kyanseru shimasho ka?
(Yoe-yah-kuu oh k'yahn-say-rue she-mah-show kah?)

Change trains - *ressha wo norikaemasu* (ray-sshah oh no-ree-kie-mahss)

You must change (trains) in Denver
Denba de ressha wo norikae nakereba narimasen
(Den-bah day ray-sshah oh no-ree-kie nah-kay-ray-bah nah-ree-mah-sin)

Coin locker - *koin rokka* (koe-een roke-kah)

The coin lockers are located next to the ticket windows
Koin rokka wa kippu uriba no tonari ni arimasu
(Coin roke-kah wa keep-puu uu-ree-bah no toe-nah-ree nee ah-ree-mahss)

Commuter pass - *teiki ken* (tay-ee-kee ken)
Conductor (ticket-checker) - *shasho* (shah-show)

May I see your ticket, please
Kippu wo haiken sasete itadakimasu
(Keep-puu oh hi-ken sah-say-tay ee-tah-dah-kee-mahss)

Departure platform - *hassha homu* (hah-sshah hoe-muu)
Dining car - *shokudo sha* (show-kuu-doe shah)

The dining car is coach number 8
Shokudo sha wa hachi go sha desu
Show-kuu-doe shah wa hah-chee go shah dess)

Elevated train - *koka tetsudo* (koe-kah tate-sue-doe)
Express - *kyuko* (que-koe)
Express ticket - *kyuko ken* (que-koe ken)
Express train - *kyuko ressha* (que-koe ray-sshah)
First train - *shi hatsu* (she haht-sue); *saisho no ressha* (sie-show no ray-sshah)
Forget - *wasuremasu* (wah-sue-ray-mahss)
Forgotten item - *wasuremono* (wah-sue-ray-moe-no)

Free-seating (not reserved) - *jiyu seki* (jee-yuu say-kee)
Information Office - *annai jo* (ahn-nie joe)
Last train - *shu den* (shuu dane); *saigo no ressha* (sie-go no ray-sshah)
Local train (stops at all stops) - *kaku eki teisha* (kah-kuu eh-kee tay-ee-shah)

This is a local train
Kore wa kaku eki teisha desu
(Koe-ray wah kah-kuu eh-kee tay-ee-shah dess)

Long-distance express train - *tokkyu* (toke-que)
Long-distance semi-express train - *kyuko* (que-koe)
Lose (something) - *nakushimasu* (nah-kuu-shee-mahss)
Lost (something) - *nakushimashita* (nah-kuu-she-mah-ssh-tah)

Have you lost something?
Nani ka nakushimashita ka?
(Nah-nee kah nah-kuu-she-mah-ssh-tah kah?)

Lost and Found Offlce - *Wasuremono Toriatsukai Jo* (Wah-sue-ray moe-no Toe-ree-aht-sue-kie Joe)

Please check with (ask) Lost and Found
Wasuremono Toriatsukai Jo ni kiite kudasai
(Wah-sue-ray-moe-no Toe-ree-aht-sue-kie Joe nee kee-ee-tay kuu-dah-sie)

Next train - *tsugi no densha* (t'sue-ghee no dane-shah)
No Smoking car - *kin'en sha* (keen-inn shah)
Physical disability - *shintai shogai* (sheen-tie show-guy)
Platform - *homu* (hoe-muu)
Porter - *pota* (poe-tah)
Reservations Office/Window - *yoyaku uketsuke no madoguchi* (yoe-yah-kuu uu-kate-sue-kay no mah-doe-guu-chee)
Reserved seat (single seat) - *yoyaku seki* (yoe-yah-kuu say-kee)

Reserved seats (whole coach) - *shitei seki* (she-tay-ee say-kee)
Reserved table - *yoyaku teburu* (yoe-yah-kuu tay-buu-rue)
Round-trip - *ofuku* (oh-fuu-kuu)
Seat belt - *zaseki beruto* (zah-say-kee bay-rue-toe)
Sleeping car - *shindai sha* (sheen-die shah)

This train has sleeping cars
Kono ressha wa shindai sha ga tsuite imasu
(Koe-no ray-sshah wa sheen-die shah ga t'sue-ee-tay ee-mahss)

Snack bar - *sunakku ba* (sue-nock-kuu bah)
Station - *eki* (eh-kee); *suteshon* (sue-tay-shone)

It is a short walk from here to the station
Koko kara eki made aruite sugu desu
(Koe-koe kah-rah eh-kee mah-day ah-rue-e-tay sue-guu dess)

The station is about minutes from here by taxi
Eki wa koko kara takushi de daitai fun desu
(Eh-kee wah koe-koe kah-rah tah-kuu-she day die-tie foon dess)

Subway- *chikatetsu* (chee-kah-tate-sue)

It is better to go by subway
Chikatetsu de iku ho ga ii desu
(Chee-kah-tate-sue day ee-kuu hoe gah ee dess)

The subway station is only a three-or four-minute walk
Chikatetsu no eki wa aruite san/yon pun dake desu
(Chee-kah-tate-sue no eh-kee wah ah-rue-ee-tay sahn/yoan
poon dah-kay dess)

Through-train - *chokutsu-ressha* (choke-sue-ray-sshah)
Ticket - *kippu* (keep-puu)

Adult ticket - *otona no kippu* (oh-toe-nah no keep-puu)
Children's ticket - *kodomo no kippu* (koe-doe-moe no keep-puu)
Express ticket - *kyuko ken* (que-koe ken)
One-way ticket - *kata-michi kippu* (kah-tah-mee-chee keep-puu)
Ordinary ticket - *josha ken* (joe-shah ken)
Roundtrip ticket - *ofuku kippu* (oh-fuu-kuu keep-puu)
Special express ticket - *tokubetsu kyuko ken* (toe-kuu-bet-sue
que-koe ken)
First-class ticket - *itto ken* (eet-toe ken)
Second-class ticket - *ni-to ken* (nee-toe ken)
Third-class ticket - *san-to ken* (sahn-toe ken)

One (ticket) - *ichi mai* (ee-chee my)
Two (tickets) - *ni mai* (nee my)
Three (tickets) - *san mai* (sahn my)
Four (tickets) - *yon mai* (yoan my)

Ticket gate - *kaisatsu guchi* (kie-saht-sue guu-chee)
Ticket office - *kippu uriba* (keep-puu uu-ree-bah)
Ticket sales (window/counter) - *kippu uriba* (keep-puu uu-ree-bah)
Ticket vending machine - *kippu hatsubai ki* (keep-puu haht-sue-by kee)
Timetable - *jikoku-hyo* (jee-koe-kuu h'yoe)

Track- *sen* (sen)

Track No. 1 - *ichiban sen* (ee-chee-bahn sen)
Track No. 2 - *niban sen* (nee-bahn sen)
Track No. 3 - *sanban sen* (sahn-bahn sen)
Track No. 4 - *yonban sen* (yoan-bahn sen)
Track No. 5 - *goban sen* (go-bahn sen)
Track No. 6 - *rokuban sen* (roe-kuu-bahn sen)

Transfer (to another train/line) - *norikaemasu* (no-ree-kie-mahss)

You must transfer at the fifth station from here
Koko kara go-bamme no eki de norikae nakereba narimasen
(Koe-koe kah-rah go-bahm-may no eh-kee day no-ree-kie nah-kay-ray-bah nah-ree-mah-sin)

Wait - *machimasu* (mah-chee-mahss)

Please wait just a bit
Shibaraku omachi kudasai
(She-bah-rah-kuu oh-mah-chee kuu-dah-sie)

Waiting room - *machiai shitsu* (mah-chee-aye sheet-sue)

Please wait in the waiting room
Machiai shitsu de matte kudasai
(Mah-chee-aye sheet-sue day maht-tay kuu-dah-sie)

Window seat - *madogawa zaseki* (mah-doh-gah-wah zah-say-kee)

Do you prefer a window seat?
Madogawa zaseki no ho ga ii desu ka?
(Mah-doe-gah-wah zah-say-kee no hoe gah ee dess kah?)

PART 2

IMMIGRATION AND CUSTOMS

Key Words & Useful Sentences

Airport tax - *kuko zei* (kuu-koe zay-ee)
American Embassy - *Amerika Taishikan* (Ah-may-ree-kah Tie-she-kahn)
Agricultural products - *nosan butsu* (no-sahn boot-sue)

Do you have any agricultural products?
Nosan butsu ga arimasu ka?
(No-sahn boot-sue gah ah-ree-mahss kah?)

Arrival/landing card - *tochaku kaado* (toe-chah-kuu kah-doe)

Please fill out your landing card
Tochaku kaado wo kinyu shite kudasaimase
(Toe-chah-kuu kah-doe oh keen-yuu ssh-tay kuu-dah-sie-mah-say)

Baggage - *nimotsu* (nee-moat-sue)

Carry-on baggage - *te-nimotsu* (tay-nee-moat-sue)

Unaccompanied baggage - *besso hin* (base-soh heen)

Is this your baggage?
Kore wa anato no nimotsu desu ka?
(Koe-ray wah ah-nah-tah no nee-moat-sue dess kah?)

Is this all (of your baggage)?
Kore wa zembu desu ka?
(Koe-ray wah zem-buu dess kah?)

Bonded area (warehouse) - *ho zei* (hoe zay-ee)

You can keep this in bond at the airport

Kuko de kore wo ho zei atsukai ni dekimasu
(Kuu-koe day koe-ray oh hoe zay-ee aht-sue-kie nee day-kee-mahss)

Citizenship - *shiminken* (she-mean-kane); *kokuseki* (koe-kuu-say-kee)
Clearance/approval - *kyoka* (k'yoe-kah)
Complete (filling out form) - *shorui wo kakioeru* (show-ruu-ee oh kah-kee-oh-eh-ruu)

Please complete this form
Kono shorui wo kakioette kudasai
(Koe-no show-rue-ee oh kah-kee-oh-eht-tay kuu-dah-sie)

Contact address - *renraku saki* (rane-rah-kuu sah-kee)

Please leave (write down) a contact address
Renraku saki wo kaite kudasai
(Rane-rah-kuu sah-kee oh kie-tay kuu-dah-sie)

Customs (customs house) - *zeikan* (zay-ee-kahn)
Customs declaration - *zeikan shinkokusho* (zay-ee-kahn sheen-koe-kuu-show)

Have you filled out a customs declaration?
Zeikan shinkokusho wo kinyu shimashita ka?
(Zay-ee-kahn sheen-koe-kuu-show oh keen-yuu she-mah-sshtah kah?)

Customs duty (fee) - *zeikin* (zay-ee-keen)

Please pay the customs fees here
Koko de zeikin wo haratte kudasai
(Koe-koe day zay-ee-keen oh hah-raht-tay kuu-dah-sie)

Customs inspection - *zeikan no kensa* (zay-ee-kahn no kane-sah)
Customs officer - *zeikan ri* (zay-ee-kahn ree)
Customs (tax) rates - *kanzei ritsu* (kahn-zay-ee reet-sue)
Customs regulations - *tsukan kisei* (t'sue-kahn kee-say-ee)
Date of birth - *sei nen gappi* (say-ee nane gahp-pee)

What is the date of your birth?
Sei nen gappi wa nan desho ka?
(Say-ee nane gahp-pee wah nahn day-show kah?)

Declare, report - *shinkoku* (sheen-koe-kuu)

Do you have anything to declare?
Shinkoku suru mono ga arimasu ka?
(Sheen-koe-kuu sue-rue moe-no gah ah-ree-mahss kah?)

Is this new?
Kore wa shinpin desu ka?
(Koe-ray wah sheen-peen dess kah?)

You must make a written dedaration
Shorui ni yoru shinkoku ga hitsuyo desu
(Show-rue-ee nee yoe-rue sheen-koe-kuu gah he-t'sue-yoe dess)

Please fill it out in ink (with a pen)
Pen de kinyu shite kudasai
(Pen day keen-yuu sshtay kuu-dah-sie)

Please keep it with your passport
Pasupoto to go-issho ni o'mochi kudasai
(Pahs-poe-toe toe go-ees-show nee oh-moe-chee kuu-dah-sie)

Diseases - *byoki* (b'yoe-kee)
Disembarkation - *nyukokukoki* (n'yuu-koe-kuu-koe-kee)

Where is your next disembarkation?
Kono tsugi no nyukokukoki wa doko desu ka?
(Koe-no t'sue-ghee no n'yuu-koe-kuu-koe-kee wah doe-koe dess kah?)

Document - *shorui* (show-rue-ee)
Drugs - *mayakurui* (mah-yah-kuu-rue-ee)

Illegal drugs are forbidden
Fuho no mayakurui wa kinjirarete imasu
(Fuu-hoe no mah-yah-kuu-rue-ee wah keen-jee-rah-ray-tay ee-mahss)

Duty (tax) - *kanzei* (kahn-zay-ee); *zeikin* (zay-ee-keen)

You must pay duty on that
Sore ni zeikin wo harawanakereba narimasen
(So-ray nee zay-ee-keen oh hah-rah-wah-nah-kay-ray-bah nah-ree-mah-sin)

Embarkation - *shukkokujoki* (shuke-koe-kuu-joe-kee)

Endangered species list - *kishodoshokubutsu risuto* (kee-show-doe-show-kuu-boot-sue rees-toe)

Entry form, card - *nyugoku shorui* (n'yuu-go-kuu show-ruu-ee)

Have you filled out an entry card?
Nyugoku kaado no go-kinyu wa o'sumi desho ka?
(N'yuu-go-kuu kall-doe no go-keen-yuu wa oh-sue-me day-show kah?)

Extension of stay - *zairyu kikan koshin* (zie-r'yuu kee-kahn koe-sheen)
Family name - *sei* (say-ee); *myoji* (m'yoejee)
Fill out - *kinyu suru* (keen-yuu sue-rue)
Firearms - *kaki* (kah-kee)
Form - *yoshi* (yoe-she)
Fruit - *kudamono* (kuu-dah-moe-no)
Given name - *na* (nah); *namae* (nah-my)
Government formalities - *shutsunyugoku tetsuzuki* (shute-sue-n'yuu-go-kuu tate-sue-zuu-kee) Immigration - *shutsunyugokukanri* (shute-suu-n'yuu-go-kuu-kahn-ree)
Immigration card - *shutsunyukoku kaado* (shute-sue-n'yuu-koe-kuu kah-doe)

Immigration Counter - *shutsunyukoku kenetsu kaunta* (shute-sue-n'yuu koe-kuu ken-eht-sue kah-oon-tah)
Immigration inspector - *shutsunyukoku kenetsu kanri* (shute-sue-n'yuu koe-kuu ken-eht-sue kahn-ree)
Immigration office - *Nyukokukanri jimusho* (N'yuu-koe-kuu-kahn-ree jeem-show)
Immigration officer - *Nyukokukan ri* (N'yuu-koe-kuu-kahn Ree)

How long will you be staying?
Dono kurai taizai shimasu ka?
(Doe-no kuu-rye tie-zie she-mahss kah?

What is the purpose of your visit?
Go-homon no mokuteki wa nan de gozaimasu ka?
(Go-hoe-moan no moe-kuu-tay-kee wah nahn day go-zie-mahss kah?)

Your documents appear to be properly filled out
Subete chanto kinyu sarete iru yo desu
(Sue-bay-tay chahn-toe keen-yuu sah-ray-tay ee-rue yoe dess)

Inspect - *kensa suru* (kane-sah sue-rue)

Inspection - *kensa* (kane-sah)

I must inspect all of your baggage
Nimotsu wo zembu kensa shinakereba narimasen
(Nee-moat-sue oh zem-buu kane-sah she-nah-kay-ray-bah nah-ree-mah-sin)

Japanese Consulate - *Nihon Ryojikan* (Nee-hoan R'yoe-jee-kahn)

I will take you to the Japanese Consulate
Nihon Ryojikan ni tsurete agemasu
(Nee-hoan R'yoe-jee-kahn nee t'sue-ray-tay ah-gay-mahss)

Japanese Embassy - *Nihon Taishikan* (Nee-hoan Tie-she-kahn)
Letter of employment - *zaishoku shomeisho* (zie-show-kuu show-may-ee show)

Letter of guarantee - *hosho sho* (hoe-show show)
Limit - *seigen* (say-ee-gane)
Luggage - *nimotsu* (nee-moat-sue)
Name - *namae* (nah-my)

Please print your name in block letters
O'namae wo katsuji tai de kaite kudasai
(Oh-nah-my oh kaht-sue-jee tie day kie-tay kuu-dah-sie)

Nationality - *kokuseki* (koe-kuu-say-kee)

What is your nationality?
Kokuseki wa doko desho ka?
(Koe-kuu-say-kee wa doe-koe day-show kah?)

Non-resident - *hiju-jusha* (he-juu-juu-shah)
Occupation - *shokugyo* (show-kuu-g'yoe)

What is your occupation?
Shokugyo wa nan desu ka?
(Show-kuu-g'yoe wah nahn dess kah?)

Open - *akemasu* (ah-kay-mahss)

Please open your briefcase
Kaban wo akete kudasai
(Kah-bahn oh ah-kay-tay kuu-dah-sie)

Oral declaration - *koto shinkoku* (koh-toh sheen-koe-kuu)

An oral declaration will be fine
Koto shinkoku wa kekko de gozaimasu
(Koe-toe sheen-koe-kuu wah keck-koe day go-zie-mahss)

Passport - *ryoken* (r'yoe-ken); *pasupoto* (pahss-poe-toe)
Passport number - *ryoken bango* (r'yoe-ken bahn-go)

Please show me your passport
Pasupoto wo misete kudasai
(Pah-sue-poe-toe oh me-say-tay kuu-dah-sie)

Permanent address - *hon seki* (hoan say-kee)

What is your permanent address?
Anata no hon seki wa nan desu ka?
(Ah-nah-tah no hoan say-kee wah nahn dess kah?)

Personal belongings/effects - *mino mawarihin* (me-no mah-wah-ree-heen)
Port of entry - *nyukoku chi* (n'yuu-koe-kuu chee)
Profession - *shokugyo* (show-kuu-g'yoe)
Quarantine - *keneki* (ken-eh-kee)
Receipt - *uketori* (uu-kay-toe-ree)

Do you have a receipt for that?
Sore ni uketori gozaimasu ka?
(Soe-ray nee uu-kay-toe-ree go-zie-mahss kah?)

Re-entry permit - *sai-nyukoku kyokasho* (sie-n'yuu-koe-kuu k'yoe kah-show)

A re-entry permit is necessary
Sai-nyukoku kyokasho wa hitsuyo desu
(Sie-n'yuu-koe-kuu k'yoe-kah-show wah he-t'sue-yoe dess)

Resident - *kyojusha* (k'yoe-juu-shah)
Resident status - *zairyu shikaku* (zie-r'yuu she-kah-kuu)
Restricted items - *seigen hin* (say-ee-gain hean)

That is a restricted item
Sore wa seigen hin desu
(Soe-ray wah say-ee-gain hean dess)

Suitcase - *sutsukesu* (sue-t'sue-kay-sue)

Please open that suitcase
Sono sutsukesu wo akete kudasai
(So-no sue-t'sue-kay-sue oh ah-kay-tay kuu-dah-sie)

Surname/last name - *sei* (say-ee); *myoji* (m'yoe-jee)

Is this your last name?
Kore wa o'myoji de gozaimasu ka?
(Koe-ray wah oh-m'yoe-jee day go-zie-mahss kah?)

Tax (duty) - *zeikin* (zay-ee-keen)
Taxable items - *kazuei kaisho bukkin* (kah-zuu-eh-ee kie-show buke-keen)

Please write down all of your taxable items
O'mochi no kazuei kaisho bukkin wo subete o'kaki kudasai
(Oh-moe-chee no kah-zuu-eh-ee kie-show buke-keen oh sue-bay-tay oh-kah-kee kuu-dah-sie)

Tax free - *mu zei* (muu zay-ee)
Tax-free shop - *mu-zei ten* (muu-zay-ee tane)

Did you buy that at a tax-free shop?
Sore wo mu-zei ten de kaimashita ka?
(So-ray oh muu-zay-ee tane day kie-mah-sshtah kah?

Tax rate - *zei ritsu* (zay-ee reet-sue)
Tobacco - *tabako* (tah-bah-koe)
Transit passenger - *tsuka ryokaku* (t'sue-kah r'yoe-kah-kuu)

Are you a transit passenger?
O'kyaku san ga tsuka ryokaku desu ka?
(Oh-k'yah-kuu sahn gah t'suu-kah r'yoe-kah-kuu dess kah?)

Travel document - *ryoko kiroku* (r'yoe-koe kee-roe-kuu)
Travel document number - *ryoko kiroku bango* (rio-koe kee-roe-kuu bahn-go)
Unaccompanied baggage - *besso hin* (base-soe heen)

Do you have any unaccompanied baggage?
Besso hin ga arimasu ka?
(Base-soe heen gah ah-ree-mahss kah?)

Vessel/ship (name of) - *sen mei* (sen-may-ee).
Visa - *bisa* (bee-sah); *sasho* (sah-show)

A visa is not necessary for a short visit
Mijikai taizai no baai ni wa bisa ga irimasen
(Mejee-kie tie-zie no bah-aye nee wah bee-sah ga ee-ree-mah-sin)

Whiskey - *uisuki* (we-ski)

How many bottles do you have?
Nan bon gozaimasu ka?
(Nahn bone go-zie-mahss kah?)

Wine - *budoshu* (buu-doe-shuu); *wainu* (wie-nuu)

PART 3

BUSES, LIMOUSINES AND TAXIS

Key Words & Useful Sentences

Private transportation - *kojin no norimono* (koe-jeen no no-ree-moe-no)
Public transportation - *kokyo no norimono* (koe-k'yoe no no-ree-moe-no)
Bus - *basu* (bah-sue)
Taxi - *takushi* (tock-she)
Subway- chikatetsu (chee-kah-tate-sue)
Streetcar, tramcar - *densha* (dane-shah)
Train - *densha* (dane-shah), *ressha* (ray-sshah)
Downtown - *shitamachi* (ssh-tah-mah-chee)*

*Shitamachi literally means "downtown," and may be used in that sense anywhere, anytime. But keep in mind that in Tokyo it is also synonymous with the old portions of the city. There are several major sections to contemporary Tokyo's "downtown" area and it is best to specify which of these areas you have in mind (the Ginza district; the Yurakucho-Hibiya area; the Marunouchi district, the Tokyo Station area, and so on). The same generally applies to other major world cities.

Within the city - *shi nai* (she nie)
Suburbs (outside the city) - *shi gai* (she guy)

BUS SERVICE

Airport shuttle (bus) - *eapoto shataru* (eh-ah-poe-toe shah-tah-rue)

The airport shuttle leaves every hour
Eapoto shataru wa ichiji-kan goto ni demasu
(Eh-ah-poe-toe shah-tah-rue wah ee-cheejee-kahn go-toe nee day-mahss)

Do you want to go by bus?
Basu de ikitai desu ka?
(Bah-sue day ee-kee-tie dess kah?)

Shall I make reservations for you?
Yoyaku wo shimasho ka?
(Yoe-yah-kuu oh she-mah-show kah?)

Board (get on the bus) - *norimasu* (no-ree-mahss)

Please get on the bus
Basu ni notte kudasai
(Bah-sue nee note-tay kuu-dah-sie)

The bus will leave at 1 o'clock
Basu ga ichiji ni demasu
(Bah-sue gah ee-cheejee nee day-mahss)

Bus boarding guide - *basu noriba annai* (bah-sue no-ree-bah ahn-nie)
Bus boarding place - *basu noriba* (bah-sue no-ree-bah)

The bus boarding place is in front of the hotel
Basu noriba wa hoteru no mae desu
(Bah-sue no-ree-bah wah hoe-tay-rue no my dess)

The shuttle bus fare is _____ dollars
Shataru basu no chaji wa _____ doru desu
(Shah-tah-rue bah-sue no chah-jee wah doe-rue dess)

Bus driver - *doraiba* (doe-rye-bah)

Please pay the driver
Doraiba ni haratte kudasai
(Doe-rye-bah nee hah-raht-tay kuu-dah-sie)

Bus service - *basu sabisu* (bah-sue sah-bee-sue)

The bus service in this city is poor
Kono machi no basu sabisu wa yokunai desu
(Koe-no mah-chee no bah-sue sah-bee-sue wah yoe-kuu-nie dess)

Buses come every 20 minutes
Basu wa nijip-pun goto ni kimasu
(Bah-sue wah nee-jeep-poon ~o-toe nee kee-mahss)

Bus fare (for city bus) - *ryokin* (r'yoe-keen); *unchin* (oon-cheen)

You will need some small change
Komakai no ga irimasu
(Koe-mah-kie no gah ee-ree-mahss)

Bus line - *basu sen* (bah-sue sen)
Bus station - *basu eki* (bah-sue eh-kee)

The bus station is in the center of town
Basu eki wa shi no chuo desu
(Bah-sue eh-kee wah she no chuu-oh dess)

Bus stop - *teiryu jo* (tay-ee-r'yuu joe); sutoppu (stope-puu)

Get off at the fi~ch stop
Go bamme no teiryu jo de orite kudasai
(Go bahm-may no tay-ee-r'yuu joe day oh-ree-tay kuu-dah-sie)

The next one is your stop
Kono tsugi wa anata no sutoppu desu
Koe-no t'sue-ghee wah ah-nah-tah no stope-puu dess)

Chartered bus - *chata basu* (chah-tah bah-sue)

We will be going by chartered bus
Chata basu de ikimasu
(Chah-tah bah-sue day ee-kee-mahss)

It will take about three hours
Sanji kan gurai kakarimasu
(Sahnjee kahn guu-rye kah-kah-ree-mahss)

Destination - *yukisaki* (yuu-kee-sah-kee)

What is your destination?
Yukisaki wa doko desu ka?
(Yuu-kee-sah-kee wah doe-koe dess kah?)

Disembark (get off) - *orimasu* (oh-ree-mahss)

When you disembark, please be careful
Oriru toki chui shite kudasai
(Oh-ree-rue toe-kee chuu-ee ssh-tay kuu-dah-sie)

End of the line - *shuten* (shuu-tane)

It is best to go all the way to the end of the line
Shuten made iku ho ga ii desu
(Shuu-tane mah-day ee-kuu hoe gah ee dess)

Last bus (of the day) - *saigo no basu* (sie-go no bah-sue)

Don't forget, the last bus leaves at midnight
Wasure nai de, saigo no basu wa yoru no juni ji desu
(Wah-sue-ray nai day, sie-go no bah-sue wah yoe-rue no juu-
nee jee dess)
Via - *keiyu* (kay-ee-yuu)

This bus goes via San Diego
Kono basu wah San Diego keiyu desu
(Koe-no bah-sue wah Sahn Dee-eh-go kay-ee-yuu dess)

LIMOUSINE SERVICE

Limousine - *rimujin* (ree-moo-jeen)
Limousine service - *rimujin sabisu* (ree-moojeen sah-bee-sue)

Yes, we have limousine service
Hai, rimujin sabisu arimasu
(Hie, ree-moo-jeen sah-bee-sue ah-ree-mahss)

Limousine charge - *rimujin chaji* (ree-moo-jeen chah-jee);
ryokin (r'yoe-keen)

The fee for one hour is _____
Ichijikan no ryokin wa _____ desu
(Ee-chee-jee-kahn no rio-kahn wah _____ dess)

The fee for one day is ___

Ichi nichi no ryokin wa _____ desu
(Ee-chee nee-chee no r'yoe-keen wa ___ dess)

How many people will be going?
Nan mei sama ga ikimasu ka?
(Nahn may-ee sah-mah gah ee-kee-mahss kah?)

Do you want it for the whole day?
Ichi nichi ju irimasu ka?
(Ee-chee nee-chee juu ee-ree-mahss kah?)

TAXI SERVICE

Taxi - *takushi* (tah-kuu-she)

Shall I call a taxi?
Takushi wo yobimasho ka?
(Tah-kuu-she oh yoe-bee-mah-show kah?)

Where do you want to go?
Doko e ikitai no desu ka?
(Doe-koe eh ee-kee-tie no dess kah?)

Are you going to the airport?
Eapoto ni ikimasu ka?
(Eh-ah-poe-toe nee ee-kee-mahss kah?)

What is your departure time?
Shuppatsu jikan wa nanji desu ka?
(Shupe-pot-sue jee-kahn wah nahn-jee dess kah?)

Don't worry. We'll get there on time
Go-shimpai naku. Jikan ni maniaimasu
(Go-sheem-pie nah-kuu. Jee-kahn nee mah-nee-aye-mahss)

Taxi fare - *takushi dai* (tah-kuu-she die)*

#Late night (taxi fare) surcharge - *yakan warimashi ryokin* (yah-kahn wah-ree-mah-she r'yoe-keen)

The taxi fare to the airport is _____
Eapoto made no takushi dai wa _____ desu
(Eh-ah-poe-toe mah-day no tah-kuu-she die wah _____ dess)

Taxi fare to the central area is about ____
Chuo made no takushi dai wa daitai ____
(Chuu-oh mah-day no tah-kuu-she die wa die-tie ____ dess)

I'll help you with your bags
Nimotsu ni tetsudai masho
(Nee-mote-sue nee tate-sue-die mah-show)

Boarding area/stand for taxis - *takushi noriba* (tah-kuu-she no-ree-bah)

Please wait at the taxi stand
Takushi noriba de matte kudasai
(Tah-kuu-she no-ree-bah day maht-tay kuu-dah-sie)

Corner - *kado* (kah-doe)
Door - *doa* (doe-ah)*

*The left rear doors of all taxis in Japan (the doors on the sidewalk side of the vehicles) are geared to open (and close) automatically when the driver flicks a switch. When they are overseas, Japanese travelers often hesitate before reaching for a taxi door handle because they expect the driver to open it . . . and they presume he prefers to open it because manually opening automated doors is not good for the mechanism.

Driver - *doraiba* (doe-rye-bah); *untenshu* (uun-tane-shuu)*

*It is common to address bus and taxi drivers as *Unten San* (Uun-tane Sahn) or "Mr./Mrs./Miss Driver."

Fast - *hayai* (hah-yie)
Freeway, expressway - *kosoku doro* (koe-soe-kuu doe-roe)

Shall we go by expressway?
Kosokudoro de ikimasho ka?
(Koe-soe-kuu doe-roe day ee-kee-mah-show kah?)

Get off/out (of vehicle) - *orimasu* (oh-ree-mahss)

Would you like to get out here?
Koko de orimasu ka?
(Koe-koe day oh-ree-mahss kah?)

Where do you want to get out?

Doko de oritai desu ka?
(Doe-koe day oh-ree-tie dess kah?)

Hurry (go/move fast) - *hayaku* (hah-yah-kuu)

Shall I go faster?
Motto hayaku ikimasho ka?
(Mote-toe hah-yah-kuu ee-kee-mah-show kah?)

Hurry (be in a hurry) - *isogimasu* (ee-so-ghee-mahss)

Are you in a hurry?
Isogimasu ka?
(Ee-so-ghee-mahss kah?)

Intersection - *kosaten* (koe-sah-tane)
Left (direction) - *hidari* (he-dah-ree)

Shall I turn to the left?
Hidari e magarimasho ka?
(He-dah-ree eh mah-gah-ree-mah-show kah?)

Let off/out (of vehicle) - *oroshimasu* (oh-roe-she-mahss)

Where shall I let you out/off?
Doko de oroshimasho ka?
(Doe-koe day oh-roe-she-mah-show kah?)

One-way street - *ippo tsuko* (eep-poe t'sue-koe)
Right (direction) - *migi* (me-ghee); right turn - *usetsu* (uu-sate-sue)

Shall I turn to the right?
Migi e magarimasho ka?
(Me-ghee eh mah-gah-ree-mah-show kah?)

There is no right turn here
Koko de usetsu dekimasen
(Koe-koe day uu-sate-sue day-kee-mah-sin)

Side road - *yoko michi* (yoe-koe mee-chee)
Side street - *yoko cho* (yoe-koe choe)
Slow - *yukkuri* (yuke-kuu-ree)
Stop - *tomarimasu* (toe-mah-ree-mahss)

Shall I stop here?

Koko de tomarimasho ka?
(Koe-koe day toe-mah-ree-mah-show kah?)

Where shall I stop?
Doko de tomarimasho ka?
(Doe-koe day toe-mah-ree-mah-show kah?)

Stoplight - *shingo* (sheen-go)
Straight - *massugu* (mahs-sue-guu)
Toll road - *yuryo doro* (yuu-r'yoe doe-roe)

Will you (passenger/guest) pay the road toll?
O'kyaku San ga yuryo doro no tsuko-ryo wo haraimasu ka?
(Oh-k'yahk Sahn gah yuu-r'yoe doe-roe no t'sue-koe-r'yoe oh
hah-rye-mahss kah?)

Turn (directions) *magarimasu* (mah-gah-ree-mahss)

I wiil let you out/off after we turn (the corner)
Magatte kara oroshimasu
(Mah-got-tay kah-rah oh-roe-she-mahss)

Please be careful
Chui shite kudasai
(Chuu-ee sshtay kuu-dah-sie)

PART 4

THE ACCOMMODATIONS INDUSTRY

Key Words & Useful Sentences

Welcome! - *Irasshaimase!* (Ee-rah-shy-mah-say!)
Hotel - *hoteru* (hoe-tay-rue)

Welcome to the _____ Hotel!
_____ *Hoteru ni irasshaimase!*
_____ Hoe-tay-rue nee ee-rah-shy-mah-say!)

Reservations - *yoyaku* (yoe-yah-kuu)

Do you have reservations?

Yoyaku shite gozaimasu ka?
(Yoe-yah-kuu sshtay go-zie-mahss kah?)

How long will you be staying?
Dono kurai go-taizai shimasu ka?
(Doe-no kuu-rye go-tie-zie she-mahss kah?)

Confirmation number - *kakunin bango* (kah-kuu-neen bahn-go)

Do you have a confirmation number?
Kakunin bango ga o'mochi desho ka?
(Kah-kuu-neen bahn-go gah oh-moe-chee day-show kah?)

Register (sign in) - *toroku shimasu* (toe-roe-kuu she-mahss)
Registration - *toroku* (toe-roe-kuu)

Please fill out this registration card
Kono toroku kado wo kinyu shite kudasai
(Koe-no toe-roe-kuu kah-doe oh keen-yuu ssh-tay kuu-dah-sie)

Address - *jusho* (juu-show)

Please write your address
Jusho wo kaite kudasai
(Juu-show oh kie-tay kuu-dah-sie)

Room - *rumu* (rue-muu); *heya* (hay-yah)

Your room is on the 4th floor. The bellboy will escort you.
O'heya wa yon kai ni arimasu. Beruboi ga go-annai shimasu.
(Oh-hay-yah wah yoan kie nee ah-ree-mahss. Bay-rue-boy gah
go-ahn-nie she-mahss.)

Your room is not quite ready. It will be ready in about 10
minutes.
*O'heya no jumbi wa mada dekite inai no desu. Ato jip pun gurai
deki agarimasu.*
(Oh-hay-yah no jume-bee wah mah-dah day-kee-tay ee-nie no
dess.
Ah-toe jeep-poon guu-rie day-kee ah-gah-ree-mahss.)

GENERAL VOCABULARY

Air conditioning - *reibo* (ray-ee-boe)

The air conditioning is already turned on
Reibo wa mo tsukete arimasu
(Ray-ee-bow wah moe t'sue-kay-tay ah-ree-mahss)

Annex - *bekkan* (bake-kahn)

Your room is in the annex
Anata sama no heya wa bekkan ni arimasu
(Ah-nah-tah sah-mah no hay-ya wah bake-kahn nee ah-ree-mahss)

Arrive - *tsukimasu* (t'ski-mahss)

When will you arrive?
Itsu tsukimasu ka?
(Eet-sue t'ski-mahss kah?)

Arrival time - *tochaku jikan* (toe-chah-kuu jee-kahn); tsuku jikan (t'sue-kuu jee-kahn)

What is your arrival time?
Tochaku no jikan wa nan desho ka?
(Toe-chah-kuu no jee-kahn wah nahn day-show kah?)

Bags (luggage) - *nimotsu* (nee-moat-sue)

Shall I send someone for your bags?
Dare ka nimotsu wo tori ni yokoshimasho ka?
(Dah-ray kah nee-moat-sue oh toe-ree nee yoe-koe-she-mah-show kah?)

Basement - *chika* (chee-kah)

1st floor down - *chika ikkai* (chee-kah eek-kie)
2nd floor down - *chika nikai* (chee-kah nee-kie)

The newsstand is in the basement
Nyuzu sutando wa chika ni arimasu
(N'yuu-zoo stahn-doe wah chee-kah nee ah-ree-mahss)

Bath - *ofuro* (oh-fuu-roe)
Bed - *beddo* (bed-doe); *shindai* (sheen-die)

King-size - *kingu saizu* (keen-guu sie-zoo)
Queen-size - *kuwin saizu* (kuu-ween sie-zoo)

Bed-and-breakfast included - *choshoku tsuki* (choe-show-kuu t'ski)
Bellboy - *beruboi* (bay-rue-boy)

I will send a bellboy immediately
Ima sugu beruboi wo yokoshimasu
(Ee-mah sue-guu bay-rue-boy oh yoe-koe-she-mahss)

Bell Desk - *beru desuku* (bay-rue dess-kuu)
Bill (list of charges) - *kanjogaki* (kahn-joe-gah-kee)
Breakfast - *asahan* (ah-sah-hahn); *choshoku* (choe-show-kuu)
Breakfast time - *asahan no jikan* (ah-sah-han no jee-kahn)

Breakfast is served from 6:30 to 9:30
Asahan wa rokuji-han kara kuji-han made desu
(Ah-sah-hahn wah roe-kuujee-hahn kah-rah kuujee mah-day dess)

Bus - *basu* (bah-sue)
Bus driver - *basu doraiba* (bah-sue doe-rie-bah)
Bus stop - *basu stoppu* (bah-sue stope-puu)

The bus stop is about two minutes from here
Basu stoppu wa koko kara daitai ni hun desu
(Bah-sue stope-puu wah koe-koe kah-rah die-tie nee hoon dess)

Business - *bijinesu* (beejee-nay-sue); *shigoto* (she-go-toe)

What business are you in?
Oshigoto wa nan desho ka?
(Oh-she-go-toe wah nahn day-show kah?)

Check-in - *chekku in* (chek-kuu een)

What time will you be checking in?
Chekku in wa nanji ni narimasu ka?
(Chek-kuu een wah nahn-jee nee nah-ree-mahss kah?)

Check-out - *chekku auto* (chek-kuu ah-uu-toe)

When will you check out?
Itsu chekku autoshimasu ka?
(Eet-sue chek-kuu ah-uu-toe she-mahss kah?)

Chef's special - *ryori-cho no o'susume hin* (r'yoe-ree-choe no oh' sue-sue-may-heen)

Cloudy- *kumotte-iru* (kuu-moat-tay-ee-rue)

Unfortunately, today is cloudy
Ainiku desu ga, kyo wa kumotte imasu
(Aye-nee-kuu dess gah, k'yoe wah kuu-mote-tay ee-mahss)

Coffee shop - *kohi shoppu* (koe-he shope-puu

The coffee shop is on the 2nd floor
Kohi shoppu wa ni-kai ni arimasu
(Koe-hee shope-puu wah nee-kie nee ah-ree-mahss)

It is open from 6 in the morning until midnight
Asa no roku ji kara yoru no juni ji made aite imasu
(Ah-sah no roe-kuu jee kah-rah yoe-rue no juu-nee jee mah-day
aye-tay ee-mahss)

Cold (to the touch) - *tsumetai* (t'sue-may-tie)

The wind is cold today
Kyo wa kaze ga tsumetai desu
(K'yoe wah kah-zay gah t'sue-may-tie dess)

Cold (weather)- *samui* (sah-muu-ee)

It is cold here from November to April
Koko wa juichi-gatsu kara shi-gatsu made samui desu
(Koe-koe wah juu-ee-chee-gaht-sue kah-rah she-gaht-sue mah-
day sah-muu-ee dess)

Credit card - *kurejitto kado* (kuu-ray-jeet-toe kah-doe)

Signature - *shomei* (show-may-ee)
American Express - *Amerikan Ekusupuresu* (Ah-may-ree-kahn
X-puu-ray-sue)
Diner's Club - *Dainasu Kurabu* (Die-nah-sue Kuu-rah-buu)
Discovery Card - *Desukabari Kado* (Dess-kah-bah-ree Kah-
doe)
MasterCard - *Masuta Kado* (Mahss-tah Kah-doe)
Visa Card - *Bisa Kado* (Bee-sah Kah-doe)

Will you be using a credit card?
Kurejitto kado wo tsukaimasu ka?
(Kuu-rayjeet-toe kah-doe oh t'sue-kie-mahss kah?)

May I have your signature, please?
Shomei wo shite kudasai
(Show-may-ee oh ssh-tay kuu-dah-sie)

Dining room - *dainingu rumu* (die-neen-guu ruu-muu); *shokudo* (show-kuu-doe)
Dinner - *yuhan* (yuu-hahn); *yushoku* (yuu-show-kuu)
Dinner time - *yuhan no jikan* (yuu-hahn no jee-kahn)

Dinner is served from 6 until 9:30
Yuhan wa roku-ji kara ku ji han made desu
(Yuu-hahn wah roe-kuu-jee kah-rah kuu-jee hahn mah-day dess)

Discount - *waribiki* (wah-ree-bee-kee)

I will give you a 10 percent discount
Ju pasento no waribiki wo shimasu
(Juu pah-sen-toe no wah-ree-bee-kee oh she-mahss)

Door / Entrance- *doa* (doe-ah); *guchi* (guu-chee)

Please use the main entrance
Shomen guchi wo tsukatte kudasai
(Show-mane guu-chee oh t'sue-kot-tay kuu-dah-sie)

Doorman - *doaman* (doe-ah-mahn)
Double room - *daburu rumu* (dah-buu-rue ruu-muu)
Elevator - *erebeta* (eh-ray-bay-tah)
Escalator - *esukareta* (ess-kah-ray-tah)
Floor (of room) - *yuka* (yuu-kah)

1st floor - ik kai (eek-kie)
2nd floor - ni kai (nee-kie)
3rd floor - san kai (sahn-kie)
4th floor - yon kai (yoan-kie)
5th floor - go kai (go-kie)
6th floor - rok kai (roke-kie)
7th floor - nana kai (nah-nah-kie)
8th floor - hachi kai (hah-chee-kie)
9th floor - kyu kai (que-kie)
10 floor - ju kai (juu kie)
11th floor - juik kai (juu-eek-kie)
12th floor - juni kai (juu-nee kie)
13th floor - jusan kai (juu-sahn kie)

14th floor - juyon kai (juu-yoan kie)
15th floor - jugo kai (juu-go kie)
16th floor - jurok kai (juu-roke kie)
17th floor - junana kai (juu-nah-nah kie)
18th floor - juhachi kai (juu-hah-chee kie)
19th floor - jukyu kai (juu-que kie)
20th floor - niju kai (nee-juu kie)

Forwarding address - *tsugi no atesaki* (t'sue-ghee no ah-tay-sah-kee)
Gift shop - *gifuto shoppu* (gheef-toe shope-puu)
Hall (hallway) - *horu* (hoe-rue)
Heat - *atsusa* (aht-sue-sah)

To heat - *atatamemasu* (ah-tah-tah-may-mahss); atsuku shimasu aht-sue-kuu she-mahss)
To heat liquids (only) - *wakashimasu* (wah-kah-she-mahss)

Shall I warm up your coffee?
Kohi wo atatamemasho ka?
(Koe-hee oh ah-tah-tah-may-mah-show kah?)

Heater - *hita* (hee-tah); *danbo-sochi* (dahn-boe-so-chee)

Shall I turn on the heater?
Hita wo tsukemasho ka?
(Hee-tah oh t'skay-mah-show kah?)

House phone - *okunai denwa* (oh-kuu-nie dane-wah)
Hot (spicy) - *karai* (kah-rie)

Do you like spicy foods?
Karai shokuji wo o'suki desu ka?
(Kah-rye show-kuujee oh oh-ski dess kah?)

Hot (to the touch) - *atsui* (aht-suu-ee)

Be careful! That's hot!
Chui shite! Sore wa atsui desu!
(Chuu-ee sshtay! Soe-ray wah aht-sue-ee dess!)

Hot (weather) - *atsui* (aht-suu-ee)

It is going to get hot today
Kyo wa atsuku narimasu
(K'yoe wah aht-sue-kuu nah-ree-mahss)

Hot water - *oyu* (oh-yuu)
Hotel safe (for valuables) - *kicho hin no kinko* (kee-choe heen no keen-koe)

Do you have anything you would like to put in the hotel safe?
Nani ka hoteru no kicho hin no kinko ni ireru mono ga arimasu ka?
(Nah-nee kah hoe-tay-rue no kee-choe heen no keen-koe nee ee-ray-rue moe-no gah ah-ree-mahss kah?)

Ice - *kori* (koh-ree); *aisu* (aye-sue)
Ice water - *aisu uota* (aye-sue woe-tah)
Laundry (soiled clothing) - *sentakumono* (sane-tah-kuu-moe-no)
Laundry service - *randori sabisu* (rahn-doe-ree sah-bee-sue)

We have laundry service every day except Sundays and holidays
Nichiyobi to kyujitsu no hoka ni randori sabisu ga mainichi arimasu
(Nee-chee-yoe-bee toe que-jeet-sue no hoe-kah nee rahn-doe-ree sah-bee-sue gah my-nee-chee ah-ree-mahss)

It (laundry/dry cleaning) will be ready by tomorrow evening
Ashita no yugata made ni deki agarimasu
(Ah-sshtah no yuu-gah-tah mah-day nee day-kee ah-gah-ree-mahss)

Lobby - *robi* (roe-bee)
Lounge - *raunji* (rah-uun-jee)

Mr. Suzuki, your guest is waiting in the lounge
Suzuki San, O'kyaku san ga raunji de matte orimasu
(Suzuki Sahn, oh-k'yahk sahn gah rah-uunjee day maht-tay oh-ree-mahss)

Lunch - *hiruhan* (he-rue-hahn); *chushoku* (chuu-show-kuu)
Lunch time - *hiruhan no jikan* (he-rue-hahn no jee-kahn)

Lunch time is from noon until 2 p.m.
Hiruhan no jikan wa ju-ni ji kara ni ji made desu
(He-rue-han no jee-kahn wah juu-nee jee kah-rah nee jee mah-day dess)

Maid - *meido* (may-ee-doe)
Maid service - *meido sabisu* (may-ee-doe sah-bee-sue)

Main building - *hon kan* (hoan kahn)

Your room is in the main building
O'heya wa hon kan ni arimasu
(Oh-hay-yah wah hoan kahn nee ah-ree-mahss)

Manager - *maneja* (mah-nayjah)

Would you like to see the manager?
Maneja ni o'me ni kakaritai no desu ka?
(Mah-nay-jahnee oh-may nee kah-kah-ree-tie no dess kah?)

Meal/meals - *shokuji* (show-kuu-jee)

With breakfast - *choshoku tsuki* (choe-show-kuu t'ski)
With meals - *shokuji tsuki* (show-kuu-jee t'ski)
Without meals - *shokuji nuki* (show-kuujee nuu-kee)

Message - *meseji* (may-say-jee)

Mr. Suzuki, there are several messages for you
Suzuki San, su messeji ga arimasu
(Sue-zoo-kee Sahn, sue may-say-jee gah ah-ree-mahss)

Mezzanine - *chunikai* (chuu-nee-kie)

The bar is on the mezzanine
Ba wa chunikai ni arimasu
(Bah wah chuu-nee-kie nee ah-ree-mahss)

Motel - *moteru* (moe-tay-rue)
Name - *namae* (nah-my)
Last name - *myoji* (m'yoe-jee)

Which (one) is your last name?
O'myoji wa dochira desho ka?
(Oh-m'yoe-jee wah doe-chee-rah day-show kah?)

Name card, business card - *meishi* (may-ee-she)

May I have one of your name cards?
Meishi wo itadakemasu ka?
(May-ee-she oh ee-tah-dah-kay-mahss kah?)

No vacancy (full) - *man shitsu* (mahn sheet-sue)

I'm sorry, there are no vacancies (we are full)
Moshi wake nai desu ga, man shitsu desu
(Moe-she-wah-kay nie dess gah, mahn sheet-sue dess)

Public telephone - *koshu denwa* (koe-shuu dane-wah)

The public phones are down that hallway
Koshu denwa wa sono horu no oku desu
(Koe-shuu dane-wah wah soe-no hoe-rue no oh-kuu dess)

Quiet - *shizukana* (she-zoo-kah-nah)

This is a very quiet place
Koko wa taihen shizukana tokoro desu
(Koe-koe wah tie-hane she-zoo-kah-nah toe-koe-roe dess)

Rain - *ame* (ah-may)

According to the weather forecast it will rain tomorrow
Tenki yoho ni yoru to ashita ame ga furimasu
(Tane-kee yoe-hoe nee yoe-rue toe ah-sshtah ah-may gah filu-ree-mahss)

Reception Desk - *uketsuke* (uu-kay-t'sue-kay)
Register - *sain suru* (sign sue-rue); *toroku suru* (toe-roe-kuu sue-rue)
Registration Desk (front desk) - *furonto* (fuu-rone-toe)

This is the front desk. May I help you?
Furonto de gozaimasu. Nani wo itashimasho ka?
(Fuu-rone-toe day go-zie-mahss. Nah-nee oh ee-tah-shemah-show kah?)

Reservations (at restaurant, etc.) - *yoyaku* (yoe-yah-kuu)

Do you have reservations?
Yoyaku shite arimasu ka?
(Yoe-yah-kuu ssh-tay ah-ree-mahss kah?)

I am sorry but we are full
Sumimasen ga, ippai desu
(Sue-me-mah-sin gah, eep-pie dess)

Shall I recommend another restaurant?
Hoka no restoran wo suisen shimasho ka?
(Hoe-kah no rays-toe-rahn oh sue-ee-sane she-mah-show kah?)

Wait just a moment please. I'll call another hotel
Chotto omachi kudasai. Hoka no hoteru ni renraku torimasu
(Choat-toe oh-mah-chee kuu-dah-sie. Hoe-kah no hoe-tay-rue
nee rane-rah-kuu toe-ree-mahss)

Room - *rumu* (rue-muu); *heya* (hay-yah)

Double - *daburu* (dah-buu-rue)
Single - *shinguru* (sheen-guu-rue)

Room rate - *heya dai* (hay-yah die)

The room rate is _____
Heya dai wa _____ *desu*
Hay-yah die wah _____ dess)

Room-and-board (room and three meals) - *sanshoku tsuki*
(sahn-show-kuu t'ski)

Room service - *rumu sabisu* (rue-muu sah-bee-sue)

Room service is available 24 hours a day
Rumu sabisu ga nijuyo jikan ni arimasu
(Rue-muu sah-bee-sue gah nee-juu-yoe jee-kahn nee ah-ree-
mahss)

Safety deposit box - *shuku kyaku yokinko* (shuu-kuu k'yah-kuu
yoe-keen-koe); *kichohin yokin ko* (kee-choe-heen yoe-keen koe)
Sales tax - *bumpin zei* (boom-peen zay-ee)
Service charge - *sabisu ryo* (sah-bee-sue r'yoe)

The service charge is included
Sabisu ryo ga haitte imasu
(Sah-bee-sue r'yoe gah hite-tay ee-mahss)

Shop (store) - *mise* (me-say)
Shopping - *kaimono* (kie-moe-no)
To go shopping - *kaimono ni ikimasu* (kie-moe-no nee ee-kee-
mahss)

Would you like to go shopping?
Kaimono ni ikitai no desu ka?
(Kie-moe-no nee ee-kee-tie no dess kah?)

Shopping arcade - *shoppingu akeido* (shope-peen-guu ah-kay-

ee-doe)
Shopping center - *shoppingu senta* (shope-peen-guu sen-tah)
Shower - *shawa* (shah-wah)
Shuttle bus - *shatoru basu* (shah-toe-rue bah-sue)

Yes, we have an airport shuttle bus
Hai, eapoto no shataru basu ga arimasu
(Hi, eh-ah-poe-toe no shah-toe-rue bah-sue gah ah-ree-mahss)

You don't need a ticket. Just pay the driver
Kippu wa irimasen. Tada doraiba ni haratte kudasai
(Keep-puu wah ee-ree-mah-sin. Tah-dah doe-rye-bah nee hah-
raht-tay kuu-dah-sie)

Sign (write your name) - *sain* (sign)

Please sign here
Koko ni sain shite kudasai
(Koe-koe nee sign ssh-tay kuu-dah-sie)

Soap - *sekken* (sake-kane)

Stay - *taizai shimasu* (tie-ee-zie-ee shee-mahss)

One night - *ippaku* (eep-pah-kuu)
Two nights - *nihaku* (nee-hah-kuu)
Three nights - *sampaku* (sahm-pah-kuu)
Four nights - *yonhaku* (yoan-hah-kuu)
Five nights - *gohaku* (go-hah-kuu)
Six nights - *roppaku* (rope-pah-kuu)
One week - *isshu kan* (ees-shuu kahn)

Summer - *natsu* (not-sue); *saama* (sah-mah)
Summer rates - *saama reito* (sah-mah ray-ee-toe)

Our summer rates start in June
Saama reito wa rokugatsu kara desu
(Sah-mah ray-ee-toe wah roe-kuu-gaht-sue kah-rah dess)

Taxes - *zeikin* (zay-ee-keen); *zei* (zay-ee)

The tax is included in the room rate
Zeikin wa heya dai ni haitte imasu
(Zay-ee-keen wah hay-yah die nee hite-tay ee-mahss)

Tax is included

Zei komi desu
(Zay-ee koe-me dess)

Taxi - *takushi* (tah-kuu-shee)
Taxi stand - *takushi noriba* (tah-kuu-shee no-ree-bah)
Telephone - *denwa* (dane-wah)

You have a telephone call
Denwa ga arimasu
(Dane-wah gah ah-ree-mahss)

Telephone operator - *denwa kokanshu* (dane-wah koe-kahn-shuu)

Telephone operator. May I help you?
Kokanshu desu. Nani wo itashimasho ka?
(Koe-kahn-shuu dess. Nah-nee oh ee-tah-she-mah-show kah?)

Time (free time) – *hima* (he-mah)

l will have free time after 5 o'clock
Goji kara hima ga arimasu
(Go-jee kah-rah hee-mah gah ah-ree-mahss)

Time (hour) - *jikan* (jee-kahn)

Together/with - *issho* (ees-show)

Please come with me
Watakushi to issho ni kite kudasai
(Wah-tock-she toe ees-show nee kee-tay kuu-dah-sie)

Towel - *taoru* (tah-oh-rue)
Twin (room) - tsuin (t'sue-een)

You should take an umbrella
Kasa wo motte iku ho ga ii desu
(Kah-sah oh mote-tay ee-kuu hoe gah ee dess)

Vacancy (available room) - *aite-iru heya* (aye-tay-ee-rue hay-yah); *ku shitsu* (kuu sheet-sue)

Yes, we have available rooms
Hai, aite-iru heya ga arimasu
(Hi, aye-tay-ee-rue hay-yah gah ah-ree-mahss)

Vacancy (sign) - *kushitsu-ari* (kuu-sheet-sue-ah-ree)
Valet service (laundry/dry cleaning) - *sentaku* (sane-tah-kuu)
Wake-up call - *wekappu koru* (way-kop-puu koe-rue); *moningu koru* (moe-neen-guu koe-rue) Weather - *tenki* (tane-kee)

Bad weather - *warui otenki* (wah-rue-ee oh-tane-kee)
Good weather - *ii otenki* (ee oh-tane-kee)
Wonderful weather - *subarashii otenki* (sue-bah-rah-she-ee oh-tane-kee)

Today the weather is going to be beautiful
Kyo no tenki wa kirei ni narimasu
(K'yoe no tane-kee wah kee-ray-ee nee nah-ree-mahss)

Welcome - *irrasshaimase* (ee-rah-shy-mah-say)

Welcome to the Miyako Hotel Tokyo
Miyako Hoteru Tokyo ni irrasshaimase
(Me-yah-koh Hoh-tay-rue Tokyo nee ee-rah-shy-mah-say)

Winter - *fuyu* (fuu-yuu); *winta* (ween-tah)
Winter rates - *fuyu no reito* (fuu-yuu no ray-ee-toe); *winta reito* (ween-tah ray-ee-toe)

PART 5

THE FOOD AND BEVERAGE INDUSTRY

Key Words & Useful Sentences

Welcome! - *Irasshaimase!* (Ee-rah-shy-mah-say!)

What would you like to have?
Nani wo itashimasho ka?
(Nah-nee oh ee-tah-she-mah-show kah?)

Drink (verb) - *nomimasu* (no-me-mahss)

What would you like to drink?
Nani wo nomitai no desu ka?
(Nah-nee oh no-me-tie no dess kah?)

Something to drink - *nomimono* (no-me-moe-no)

Would you like something to drink?
O'nomimono wa ikaga desho ka?
(Oh-no-me-moe-no wah ee-kah-gah day-show kah?)

Eat - *tabemasu* (tah-bay-mahss)
Want to eat - *tabetai* (tah-bay-tie)

What would you like to eat?
Nani wo tabetai no desu ka?
(Nah-nee oh tah-bay-tie no dess kah?)

Something to eat - *tabemono* (tah-bay-moe-no)

Would you like something to eat?
Nani ka o'tabemono wa ikaga desho ka?
(Nah-nee kah oh'tah-bay-moe-no wah ee-kah-gah day-show
kah?)

Food - *tabemono* (tah-bay-moe-no)
Meal (food) - *shokuji* (show-kuu-jee)
A la carte - *okonomi de* (oh-koe-no-me day)
Set meal - *tei shoku* (tay-ee show-kuu)

Western-style food - *Yo-shoku* (yoe-show-kuu)
Japanese-style food - *Nihon-shoku* (nee-hoan-show-kuu)

Which do you prefer? Western-style food or Japanese-style
food?
Dochira no ho ga ii desu ka? Yo-shoku ka Nihon-shoku?
(Doe-chee-rah no hoe gah ee dess kah?
Yoe-show-kuu kah Nee-hoan-show-kuu?)

Hungry - *onaka ga sukimasu* (oh-nah-kah gah ski-mahss)
Thirsty - *nodo ga kawakimasu* (no-doe gah kah-wah-kee-mahss)

Are you hungry?
Onaka ga sukimashita ka?
(Oh-nah-kah gah ski-mah-sshtah kah?)

Are you thirsty?
Nodo ga kawakimashita ka?
(No-doe gah kah-wah-kee-mah-sshtah kah?)

Separate - *betsu no* (bate-sue no)

Separate checks?
Betsu no chekku desu ka?
(Bate-sue no check-ku dess kah?)

All on one check (all together)?
Chekku wa issho desu ka?
(Check-kuu wah ees-show dess kah?)

GENERAL VOCABULARY

Appetite - *shokuyoku* (show-kuu-yoe-kuu)
Small appetite (small eater) - *sho-shoku* (show-show-kuu)
Appetizer - *zensai* (zen-sie)

How about an appetizer?
Zensai wa ikaga desho ka?
(Zen-sie wa ee-kah-gah day-show kah?)

Bar - *baa* (bah)

The bar opens at 11 o'clock
Ba wa ju-ichi ji ni akemasu
(Bah wah juu-ee-chee jee nee ah-kay-mahss)

Barbecue - *babekyu* (bah-bay-que)
Beer garden - *biya gaden* (bee-yah gah-dane)

Bill - *okanjo* (oh-kahn-joe)
Bitter (to the taste) - *nigai* (nee-guy)
Bottle - *bin* (bean)

One bottle - *ippon* (eep-pone)
Two bottles - *nihon* (nee-hone)
Three bottles - *sambon* (sahm-bone)

Box lunch - *o'bento* (oh-bane-toe)
Breakfast - *asahan* (ah-sah-hahn); *choshoku* (choe-show-kuu)
Cabaret - *kyabare* (k'yah-bah-ray)
Chair - *isu* (ee-sue)
Check (bill) - *o'kanjo* (oh-kahn-joe)
Chopsticks - *o'hashi* (oh-hah-she)

Would you like to have chopsticks?

O'hashi wa ikaga desu ka?
(Oh-hah-she wah ee-kah-gah dess kah?)

Close - *shimemasu* (she-may-mahss)

We close at 7 o'clock
Shichi ji ni shimemasu
(She-chee jee nee she-may-mahss)

Closed - *shimatte imasu* (she-mot-tay ee-mahss)

I'm sorry, but we are closed
Sumimasen ga, shimatte imasu
(Sue-me-mah-sin gah, she-maht-tay ee-mahss)

Coffee - *kohi* (koe-hee)

Would you like some coffee?
Kohi wa ikaga desho ka?
(Koe-hee wah ee-kah-gah day-show kah?)

Do you take cream and sugar?
Kurimu to o'sato wo o'ire ni narimasu ka?
(Kuu-ree-muu toe oh-sah-toe oh oh-ee-ray nee nah-ree-mahss
kah?

Shall I bring you a fresh cup of coffee?
Kohi atarashii no wo mochi itashimasho ka?
(Koe-hee ah-tah-rah-she-ee no oh moe-chee ee-tah-she-mah-
show kah?)

Coffee shop - *kohi shoppu* (koe-hee shope-puu)

Cook - *kokku* (koke-kuu)

To cook - *ryori shimasu* (r'yoe-ree she-mahss)

Delicious/good - *oishii* (oh-ee-she-ee)
Dessert - *dezato* (day-zah-toe)

Would you care for dessert?
Dezato wa ikaga desho ka?
(Day-zah-toe wah ee-kah-gah day-show kah?)

Dining room - *shoku do* (show-kuu doe); *dainingu rumu* (die-
neen-guu rue-muu)

The dining room opens at 11:30
Shoku do wa ju-ichi ji han ni akemasu
(Show-kuu doe wah juu-ee-chee jee hahn nee ah-kay-mahss)

Dinner - *yuhan* (yuu-hahn); *yushoku* (yuu-show-kuu)

One person? - *hitori desu ka?* (ssh-toe-ree dess kah?)
Two persons? - *futari desu ka?* (fuu-tah-ree dess kah?)
Three persons? - *san nin desu ka?* (sahn neen dess kah?)

How many persons (in your party)?
Nan mei sama desu ka?
(Nahn may-ee sah-mah dess kah?)

Do you have reservations?
Yoyaku ga gozaimasu ka?
(Yoe-yah-kuu gah go-zie-mahss kah?)

What name (are the reservations under)?
Onamae wa?
(Oh-nah-my wah?)

Would you like a table near the window?
Mado no soba no teburu wa ikaga desu ka?
(Mah-doe no so-bah no tay-buu-rue wah ee-kah-gah dess kah?)

Will a corner table be all right?
Sumi no teburu wa yoroshii desho ka?
(Sue-me no tay-buu-rue wah yoe-roe-she-ee day-show kah?)

Will a booth be all right?
Busu wa yoroshii desho ka?
(Buu-suu wa yoe-roe-she-ee day-show kah?)

Would you like to sit outside?
Soto de suwaritai desu ka?
(So-toe day suu-wah-ree-tie dess kah?)

This way, please
Kochira e, dozo
(Koe-chee-rah eh, doe-zoe)

Would you like something to drink first?
Saisho nanika o'nomimono wa ikaga desu ka?
(Sie-show nah-nee-kah oh-no-me-moe-no wah ee-kah-gah dess

kah?)

Have you decided (on what you want to order)?
O'kimari de gozaimasu ka?
(Oh'kee-mah-ree day go-zie-mahss kah?)

May I take your order?/What would you like to have?
Nani wo itashimasho ka?
(Nah-nee oh ee-tah-she-mah-show kah?)

Please pay the cashier
Kaikei de haratte kudasai
(Kie-kay-ee day hah-rot-tay kuu-dah-sie)

Are you going to eat it here (at a fast food place)?
Koko de meshi agarimasu ka?
(Koe-koe day may-she ah-gah-ree-mahss kah?)

Empty - *kara no* (kah-rah no)
Fork - *foku* (foh-kuu); also pronounced "hoe-kuu"
Glass - *koppu* (kope-puu)
Hand/face towel - *oshibori* (oh-she-boe-ree)*

*It is the custom in many Japanese restaurants and drinking places to give newly arrived customers small, dampened towels that are chilled in the summer and heated in the winter. Some eating and drinking places abroad have adopted this wonderfill custom.

Hot (to the touch) - *atsui* (aht-sue-ee)

The plate is very hot! Be careful!
Sara wa taihen atsui desu! Chui shite!
(Sah-rah wa tie-hane aht-sue-e dess! Chuu-ee ssh-tay!)

Hot (spicy) – *karai* (kah-rye)

It is not very spicy
Son nani karai dewa arimasen
(Soan nah-nee kah-rye day-wah ah-ree-mah-sin)

Knife - *naifu* (nie-fuu)
Light meal - *kei shoku* (kay-ee show-kuu)
Lounge - *raunji* (rah-uunjee)

Lunch - *hiruhan* (he-rue-hahn); *chushoku* (chuu-show-kuu);

ranchi (rahn-chee)
Main course - *shu han* (shuu hahn)
Medium - *mejiumu* (may-jee-uu-muu); futsu (fute-sue)
Medium-well - *mejiumu weru* (may-jee-uu-muu way-rue)
Menu - *menyu* (main-yuu)
Napkin - *napukin* (nah-puu-keen)
Open - *aite imasu* (aye-tay ee-mahss)
Open (for business sign) - *eigyo chu* (egg-yoe chuu)
Out of- *nakunatte imasu* (nah-kuu-not-tay ee-mahss)
Pepper - *kosho* (koe-show)
Plate - *sara* (sah-rah)

May I take away your plate/dishes?
O'sara wo sage shite mo yoroshii de gozaimasu ka?
(Oh-sah-rah oh sah-gay ssh-tay moe yoe-roe-she-ee day go-zie-
mahss kah?)

Rare (under-cooked) - *nama-yaki* (nah-mah-yah-kee); *rea* (ray-
ah)

How would you like it cooked?
Dono yo ni oyakishimasho ka?
(Doe-no yoh nee oh-yah-kee-she-mah-show kah?)

Recommend - *suisen shimasu* (sue-ee-sin she-mahss), susumeru
(sue-sue-may-rue)

I recommend the fish
Sakana wo suisen shimasu
(Sah-kah-nah oh sue-ee-sin she-mahss)

Recommendation, advice - *susume* (sue-sue-may)

Today's recommendation is roast beef
Honjitsu no susume wa rosu bifu de gozaimasu
(Hone-jeet-sue no sue-sue-may wah roe-sue bee-fuu day go-zie-
mahss)

Salt - *shio* (she-oh)
Salty (same as spicy) - *karai* (kah-rye)
Sauce - *sosu* (so-sue)
Saucer - *kozara* (koe-zah-rah)
Separate checks - *betsu-betsu no chekku* (bate-sue-bate-sue no
chek-kuu)

Shall I put it (your orders) on separate checks?

O'kanjo wa betsu-betsu ni shimasho ka?
(Oh-kahn-joe wa bate-sue-bate-sue nee she-mah-show kah?)

Share a table - *aiseki* (aye-say-kee)

Would you mind sharing a table?
Aiseki demo yoroshii de gozaimasu ka?
(Aye-say-kee day-moe yoe-roe-she-ee day go-zie-mahss kah?)

Sold out - *urikirashite imasu* (uu-ree-kee-rah-sshtay ee-mahss)
Snack - *sunakku* (sue-nahk-kuu)
Snack bar - *sunakku ba* (sue-nahk-kuu bah)
Sour - *suppai* (supe-pie)
Spoon - *supun* (sue-poon)
Strong/thick - *koi* (koy)
Sweet - *amai* (ah-my)
Table - *teburu* (tay-buu-rue)

Corner table - *sumi no teburu* (sue-me no tay-buu-rue)
Outside table - *omote no teburu* (oh-moe-tay no tay-buu-rue)
Terrace table - *terasu no teburu* (tay-rah-sue no tay-buu-rue)
Window table - *mado no soba no teburu* (mah-doe no so-bah no tay-buu-rue)
Toothpick - *tsumayoji* (t'sue-mah-yoe-jee)
Weak/thin - *usui* (uu-sue-ee)
Well-done (cooked thoroughly) - *yoku yaita* (yoe-kuu yie-tah)

Do you prefer it well-done?
Yoku yaita ho ga ii desu ka?
(Yoe-kuu yie-tah hoe gah ee dess kah?)

FOOD ITEMS AND COOKING STYLES

Almonds - *amondo* (ah-moan-doe)
Anchovies - *anchobi* (ahn-choe-bee)
Aperitif- *aperitifu* (ah-pay-ree-tee-fuu)
Apple - *ringo* (reen-go)
Apple pie - *appuru pai* (ahp-puu-rue pie)
Apricots - *anzu* (ahn-zoo)
Asparagus tips - *asuparagasu* (ah-sue-pah-rah-gah-sue)
Artichokes - *kiku-imo* (kee-kuu-ee-moe)
Bacon - *bekon* (bay-kone)
Baked - *tempiyakishita* (tame-pee-yah-kee-ssh-tah)
Banana - *banana* (bah-nah-nah)
Barbecued - *babekyushita* (bah-bay-que-ssh-tah)

Beans - *mame* (mah-may)
Beef- *bifu* (bee-fuu)
Beer - *biiru* (bee-rue)
Beets - *tensai* (ten-sie)
Biscuit - *bisuketto* (bee-suu-kate-toe)
Boiled - *nita* (nee-tah)
Braised - *torobi de nita* (toe-roe-bee day nee-tah)
Bread - *pan* (pahn); *buredo* (buu-ray-doe)
Broiled - *kogashita* (koe-gah-ssh-tah)
Brussel sprouts - *me-kyabetsu* (may-k'yah-bate-sue)
Butter - *bata* (bah-tah)
Cabbage - *kyabetsu* (k'yah-bate-sue)
Cake - *keki* (kay-kee)
Carrots - *ninjin* (neen-jeen)
Cauliflower - *karifurawa* (kah-ree-fuu-rah-wah)
Caviar - *kyabia* (k'yah-bee-ah)
Celery - *serori* (say-roe-ree)
Cheese - *chizu* (chee-zoo)
Cherries - *sakuranbo* (sah-kuu-rahn-boe)
Chestnuts - *kuri* (kuu-ree)
Chicken - *niwatori* (nee-wah-toe-ree); *chikin* (chee-keen)
Chicken breast - c*hikin no mune niku* (chee-keen no muu-nay nee-kuu)

Fried chicken - *furaido chikin* (fuu-rye-doe chee-keen)
Roast chicken - *rosuto chikin* (roe-suu-toe chee-keen)
Chocolate - *chokoreto* (choe-koe-ray-toe)
Chocolate cake - *chokoreto keki* (choe-koe-ray-toe kay-kee)
Chocolate ice cream - *chokoreto aisu kurimu* (choe-koe-ray-toe ice-kuu-ree-muu)
Chocolate pudding - *chokoreto pudingu* (choe-koe-ray-toe puu-deen-guu)
Chocolate sundae - *chokoreto sande* (choe-koe-ray-toe sahn-day)
Clams - *hamaguri* (hah-mah-guu-ree)
Coconut - *yashi no mi* (yah-she no me); *kokonatsu* (koe-koe-not-sue)
Codfish - *tara* (tah-rah)
Coffee - *kohi* (koe-he)
Corn-on-the-cob - *tomorokoshi* (toe-moe-roe-koe-she)
Crabmeat - *kani* (kah-nee)
Cream - *kurimu* (kuu-ree-muu)
Creamed - *kurimu ni* (kuu-ree-muu nee)
Cucumber - *kyuri* (que-ree)
Dates - *natsumeyashi* (not-sue-may-yah-she)
Dried seaweed - *nori* (no-ree)

Duck - *ahiru* (ah-he-rue)

Eggplant - *nasu* (nah-sue)
Eggs - *tamago* (tah-mah-go)
Eel - *unagi* (uu-nah-ghee)
En casserole - *do nabe de nita* (doe nah-bay day nee-tah)
Figs - *ichijiku* (ee-cheejee-kuu)
Fish - *sakana* (sah-kah-nah)
Fried - *ageta* (ah-gay-tah); furai (fuu-rye)
Fruit - *kudamono* (kuu-dah-moe-no)
Fruit juice - *furutsu jusu* (fuu-root-sue juu-sue)
Garlic - *ninniku* (neen-nee-kuu)
Glass of water - *mizu ippai* (mizu eep-pie)
Grapefruit - *gurepu furutsu* (guu-ray-puu fuu-root-sue)
Grape juice - *gurepu jusu* (guu-ray-puu juu-sue)
Grapes - *budo* (buu-doe)
Grilled - *yaita* (ya-ee-tah)
Halibut - *hirame* (he-rah-may)

Ham - *hamu* (hah-muu)
Hamburger - *hanbaga* (hahn-bah-gah)
Hazelnuts - *hashibami no mi* (hah-she-bah-me no me)
Hors d'oeuvres - *odoburu* (oh-doe-buu-rue)
Horse mackerel - *maji* (mahh-jee)
Horseradish (Western style) - *seiyo wasabi* (say-ee-yoe wah-sah-bee)
Hotdog - *hotto doggu* (hot-toe doe-guu)

Ice cream - *aisukurimu* (ice kuu-ree-muu)
Vanilla - *banira* (bah-nee-rah)
Chocolate - *chokoreto* (choe-koe-ray-toe)
Mint - *minto* (meen-toe)
Peach - *momo* (moe-moe)
Strawberry - *ichigo* (ee-chee-go)
Walnut - *kurumi* (kuu-rue-me)

Ketchup - *kechappu* (kay-chop-puu)
Lamb - *kohitsuji* (koe-heet-sue-jee)
Lamb chops - *kohitsuji no honetsuki abara niku* (koe-heet-sue-jee no hoe-nay t'ski ah-bah-rah nee-kuu); *ram choppu* (rahm chope-puu)
Leeks - *negi* (nay-ghee)
Lemon - *remon* (ray-moan)
Lemonade - *remonado* (ray-moe-nah-doe)
Lentils - *renzu-mame* (ren-zoo-mah-may)
Lettuce - *retasu* (ray-tah-sue)

Lobster - *ise ebi* (ee-say eh-bee)
Mackerel - *saba* (sah-bah)
Meat - *niku* (nee-kuu)

Medium (cooked) - *mejium* (may-jee-uum); futsu (fute-sue)
Melon - *meron* (may-roan)
Milk- *miruku* (me-rue-kuu)
Milk shake - *miruku seki* (me-rue-kuu say-kee)
Mineral water - *minearu uota* (me-nay-ah-rue woe-tah)
Mixed vegetables - *yasai moriawase* (yah-sie moe-ree-ah-wah-say)
Mushrooms - *masshurumu* (mahssh-ruu-muu)

Mustard - *masutado* (mah-sue-tah-doe); *karashi* (kah-rah-she)
Oil - *abura* (ah-buu-rah)
Olives - *oribu* (oh-ree-buu)
Onions - *tamanegi* (tah-mah-nay-ghee)
Oranges - *orenji* (oh-ren-jee)
Orange juice - *orenji jusu* (oh-ran-jee juu-sue)
Oysters - *kaki* (kah-kee)
Parsley - *paseri* (pah-say-ree)
Pastries - *o'kashi* (oh-kah-she)
Peach - *momo* (moe-moe)
Peanuts - *pinatsu* (pee-naht-sue); *nanki mame* (nahn-kee mah-may)
Pears - *nashi* (nah-she)
Peas - *endo-mame* (inn-doe-mah-may)
Pepper - *kosho* (koe-show)
Pepsi Cola - *pepushi kora* (peh-puu-she koe-rah)
Persimmon - *kaki* (kah-kee)
Pheasant - *kiji* (kee-jee)

Pie - *pai* (pie)
Apple pie - appuru pai (ahp-puu-ruu pie)
Banana pie - banana pai (bah-nah-nah pie)
Blueberry pie - *buruberi pai* (buu-rue-bay-ree pie)
Chocolate cream pie - *chokoreto kurimu pai* (choe-koe-ray-toe kuu-ree-muu pie)
Custard pie - *kusutado pai* (kahss-tah-doe pie)
Lemon cream pie - *remon kurimu pai* (ray-moan kuu-ree-muu pie)
Peach pie - *pichi pai* (pee-chee pie)

Pimiento - *piiman* (pee-mahn)
Pineapple - *painapuru* (pine-ahp-puu-rue)
Pineapple juice - *painapuru jusu* (pine-ahp-puu-rue juu-sue)

Plums - *puramu* (puu-rah-muu)
Pork - *buta niku* (buu-tah nee-kuu); *poku* (poe-kuu)
Pork chops - *buta no honetsuki abara niku* (buu-tah no hoe-nay-t'ski ah-bah-rah nee-kuu); *poku choppu* (poe-kuu chope-puu)

Pot roast - *nabeyaki ni shita* (nah-bay-yah-kee nee ssh-tah)
Potatoes - *poteto* (poe-tay-toe); *jagaimo* (jah-guy-moe)
Prawns - *kuruma ebi* (kuu-rue-mah eh-bee)
Prunes - *hoshi sumono* (hoe-she suu-moe-no); *puramu* (puu-rah-muu)
Radish - *radishi* (rah-dee-she); *aka-daikon* (ah-kah-die-kone)
Raspberries - *kiichigo* (kee-ee-chee-go)
Rice (uncooked) - *kome* (koe-may)
Rice (boiled) - *gohan* (go-hahn)
Roast beef- *rosuto bifu* (roe-suu-toe bee-fuu)
Roast pork - *rosuto poku* (roe-suu-toe poe-kuu)
Roe - *sakana no tamago* (sah-kah-nah no tah-mah-go)
Rolls (bread) - *roru pan* (roe-rue pahn)
Salad - *sarada* (sah-rah-dah)
Salmon - *shake* (shah-kay); *samon* (sah-moan)
Salt - *shio* (she-oh)
Sandwich - *sandoittchi* (sahn-doe-eet-chee); *sando* (sahn-doh)
Sardines - *iwashi* (ee-wah-she)

Sausage - *soseji* (so-say-jee)
Scallops - *hotategai* (hoe-tah-tay-guy)
Seasoning - *chomiryo* (choe-me-r'yoe)
Shellfish - *ebi rui* (eh-bee rue-ee)
Shrimp - *ko ebi* (koe eh-bee)
Snack - *sunakku* (sue-nock-kuu)
Soft drink - *sofuto dorinku* (soe-fuu-toe doe-reen-kuu)
Sole - *shitabirame* (ssh-tah-bee-rah-may)
Soup - *supu* (sue-puu)
Spaghetti - *supagetti* (spah-geht-tee)

Steak - *suteki* (sue-tay-kee)
Chateaubriand - *chatoburian* (chah-toe-buu-ree-ahn)
Filet mignon - *hire* (he-ray)
Rib-steak/T-bone - *abara niku* (ah-bah-rah nee-kuu)
Sirloin - *saroin* (sah-roe-een)

Stew - *shichu* (ssh-chuu)
Stewed - *shichu shita* (ssh-chuu ssh-tah)
Strawberries - *ichigo* (ee-chee-go)
Sugar - *sato* (sah-toe)
Sweet corn - *mochi-tomorokoshi* (moe-chee-toe-moe-roe-koe-

she); *suito kon* (suu-we-toe kone) Sweets (candy) - *kyandi* (k'yahn-dee)
Tangerine - *mikan* (me-kahn)

Tea (brown/black) - *kocha* (koe-chah)
Green tea aapanese style) - *Nihon cha* (Nee-hoan chah)
Lemon tea (brown) - *remon ti* (ray-moan tee)
Tea with milk - *miruku ti* (me-rue-kuu tee)

Toast- *tosuto* (toas-toe)
Tomatoes - *tomato* (toe-mah-toe)
Tomato juice - *tomato jusu* (toe-mah-toe juu-sue)
Tonic water - *tonikku uota* (toe-neek-kuu woe-tah)
Trout - *masu* (mah-sue)
Tuna fish - *maguro* (mah-guu-roe)
Turkey - *shichimencho* (she-chee-mane-choe); *taaki* (tah-kee)
Veal - *koushi* (koe-uu-she)
Veal cutlet - *koushi no rosu niku* (koe-uu-she no roe-suu nee-kuu)
Vegetables - *yasai* (yah-sie)
Vinegar - *su* (sue)
Waffles - *waffuru* (wahf-fuu-rue)
Walnuts - *kurumi* (kuu-rue-me)
Water - *mizu* (me-zoo)
Watercress - *kureson* (kuu-ray-soan)
Watermelon - *suika* (sue-ee-kah)
Zucchini - *kabocha* (kah-boe-chah)

ALCOHOLIC DRINKS

Alcohol - *arukoru* (ah-rue-koe-rue)
Ale - *eru* (ay-rue)
Beer - *biiru* (bee-rue)
Bottle - *bin* (bean)

How many bottles (would you like)?
Nan bon desho ka?
(Nahn bone day-show kah?)

Glass - *gurasu ippai* (guu-rah-sue eep-pie)

Double - *daburu* (dah-buu-rue)
Single - *shinguru* (sheen-guu-rue)

Bottle or glass (draft)?

Bin desu ka gurasu desu ka?
(Bean dess kah guu-rah-sue dess kah?)

Brandy - *burande* (buu-rahn-day)
Champagne - *shanpen* (shahn-pane)
Cognac - *konnyakku* (kone-yahk-kuu)
Daiquiri - *daikuri* (die-kuu-ree)
Draft beer - *nama biiru* (nah-mah bee-rue)

We have three kinds of draft beer
San shurui no nama biiru ga arimasu
(Sahn shuu-rue-ee no nah-mah bee-rue gah ah-ree-mahss)

Gin - *jin* (jeen)
Ginger ale - *jinja eru* (jeen-jah ay-rue)
Gin fizz - *jin fizu* (jeen fee-zoo)
Gin and tonic - *jin tonikku* (jeen toe-neek-kuu)
Liqueur - *rikyuru* (ree-que-rue)
Liquor - *shu* (shuu)
Non-alcoholic - *arukoru nashi* (ah-rue-koe-rue nah-she)
On-the-rocks - *on-za-rokku* (own-zah-roke-kuu)
Port wine - *poto wain* (poe-toe wine)
Refill - *okawari* (oh-kah-wah-ree)
Rum - *ramu* (rah-muu)
Scotch - *sukochi* (sue-koe-chee)
Sherry - *sheri* (shay-ree)
Soft drink - *sofuto dorinku* (soe-fuu-toe doe-reen-kuu)
Tequila - *tekira* (tay-kee-rah)
Vermouth - *berumotto* (bay-rue-moat-toe)
Vodka - *uokka* (woke-kah)

Screwdriver - *sukuru doraiba* (sue-kuu-rue doe-rye-bah)

Whiskey - *uisuki* (we-ski)

Whiskey neat/straight - *uisuki on za rokku* (we-ski own-zah roke-kuu)
Whiskey and soda - *haiboru* (hie-boe-rue)
Wine - *budoshu* (buu-doe-shuu); *wainu* (wie-nuu)
Wine list - *wain risuto* (wine rees-toe)

PART 6

THE RETAIL STORE TRADE

Key Words & Useful Sentences

Welcome! - *Irasshaimase*! (Ee-rah-shy-mah-say!)
Good morning - *ohayo gozaimasu* (oh-hah-yoe go-zie-mahss)
Good afternoon - *konnichi wa* (kone-nee-chee wah)
Good evening - *konban wa* (kone-bahn wah)

May I help you?
Nani wo itashimasho ka?
(Nah-nee oh ee-tah-she-mah-show kah?)

SHOP TALK

Accept (money from customer) - *azukari* (ah-zoo-kah-ree)*

*Azukari literally means "to take custody of." It is customary in Japan for storekeepers and others who accept money from customers to repeat the amount of money they receive (to avoid mistakes). If they are handed one thousand yen, for example, they say: *Sen en o' azukari shimasu* (sen inn oh-ah-zoo-kah-ree she-mahss). In other words, "I have taken custody of your one thousand yen."

Address (for mailing packages) - *jusho* (juu-show)

Please write your name and address
Namae to jusho wo kaite kudasai
(Nah-my toe juu-show oh kie-tay kuu-dah-sie)

Arcade - *akeido* (ah-kay-ee-doe)
Bag - *fukuro* (fuu-kuu-roe); *baggu* (bahg-guu)

Paper bag - *kami bukuro* (kah-me buu-kuu-roe)
Plastic bag - *purasuchiku* (puu-rahss-chee-kuu)
Designer bag - *burando mo no baggu* (buu-rahn-doe moe no bahg-guu)

Bakery - *pan-ya* (pahn-yah)
Barber - *Toko-ya* (toe-koe-yah)
Bargain - *bagen* (bah-gain)

Bargain sale - *bagen seru* (bah-gain say-rue)
Book store - *hon ya* (hoan yah)
Box - hako (hah-koe)

Brand - *burando* (buu-rahn-doe)
Business hours - *eigyo jikan* (egg-yoe jee-kahn)
Change - *o'tsuri* (oh-t'sue-ree)*

*This is the "change" you get back when you give the cashier a larger amount than what you actually owe.

Closed - *shimatte imasu* (she-mot-tay ee-mahss)
Clothing store - *yofuku ya* (yofe-kuu yah)
Counter - *kaunta* (kah-uun-tah)
Country of origin - *gensan koku mei* (gane-sahn koe-kuu may-ee)
Credit card - *kurejitto kado* (kuu-rayjeet-toe kah-doe)

Yes, we accept credit cards
Hai, kurejitto kado wo uketorimasu
(Hi, kuu-ray-jeet-toe kah-doe oh uu-kay-toe-ree-mahss)

Deliver - *todokemasu* (toe-doe-kay-mahss)

We will delivery it to your hotel this afternoon
Kyo gogo hoteru ni todokemasu
(K'yoe go-go hoe-tay-rue nee toe-doe-kay-mahss)

Delivery (service) - *haitatsu* (hi-tot-sue)

I'm sorry, we cannot deliver it
Moshiwake nai desu ga, haitatsu dekimasen
(Moe-she-wah-kay nie dess gah, hi-tot-tsue day-kee-mah-sin)

Department store - *depato* (day-pah-toe)
Domestic product (not imported) - *kokusan* (koe-kuu-sahn)

This is a domestic product; not an import
Kore wa kokusan desu; yunyu shita mono de wa arimasen
(Koe-ray wah koe-kuu-sahn dess; yune-yuu ssh-tah moe-no day-wah ah-ree-mah-sin)

Drugstore - *kusuri-ya* (kuu-sue-ree-yah)

There is a drugstore in the basement

Kusuri-ya wa chikani arimasu
(Kuu-sue-ree-yah wah chee-kahnee ah-ree-mahss)

Electric appliance store - *denki ya* (dane-kee yah)
Exchange (a product) - *torikaemasu* (toe-ree-kie-mahss); *kokan* (koe-kahn)

Yes, we can exchange it
Hai, kokan dekimasu
(Hi, koe-kahn day-kee-mahss)

Fit (right size) - *aimasu* (aye-mahss)

It fits (you) perfectly
Pittari aimasu
(Peet-tah-ree aye-mahss)

Do the shoes fit?
Kutsu ga aimasu ka?
(Koot-sue gah aye-mahss kah?)

Folk craft - *mingei hin* (mean-gay-ee heen)
Furniture store - *kagu ya* (kah-guu yah)
Gift - *omiyage* (oh-me-yah-gay); *okurimono* (oh-kuu-ree-moe-no)
Go shopping - *kaimono ni ikimasu* (kie-moe-no nee ee-kee-mahss)
Grams - *guramu* (guu-rah-muu)
Hand-bag - *hando baggu* (hahn-doe bahg-guu)
Hand-made- *te-zukuri* (tay-zoo-kuu-ree)
Have - *arimasu* (ah-ree-mahss)

Do not have - *arimasen* (ah-ree-mah-sen)

Hours (the store is open) - *eigyo jikan* (egg-yoe jee-kahn)

We are open from 10 a.m. until 9 p.m.
Eigyo jikan wa gozen no juji kara yoru no kuji made desu
(Egg-yoe jee-kahn wah go-zane no juujee kah-rah yoe-rue no kuujee mah-day dess)

Imported - *yunyu no* (yune-yuu no)
Instructions (how to assemble/operate) - *setsumeisho* (sate-sue-may-ee-show)
Made in China - *Chugoku sei* (Chuu-go-kuu say-ee)

This is made in China
Kore wa Chugoku sei desu
(Koe-ray wah Chuu-go-kuu say-ee dess)

Made in England - *Eikoku sei* (Ay-ee-koe-kuu say-ee)
Made in France - *Furansu sei* (Fuu-rahn-sue say-ee)
Made in Germany - *Doitsu sei* (Doe-eet-sue say-ee)
Made in Italy - *Itaria sei* (Ee-tah-ree-ah say-ee)
Made in Korea - *Kankoku sei* (Kahn-koe-kuu say-ee)
Made in Taiwan - *Taiwan sei* (Tie-wahn say-ee)
Made in the U.S. - *Amerika sei* (Ah-may-ree-kah say-ee)

Mail (send) - *okurimasu* (oh-kuu-ree-mahss)

Shall I mail this to Japan (for you)?
Kore wo Nihon made okurimasho ka?
(Koe-ray oh Nee-hoan mah-day oh-kuu-ree-mah-show kah?)

Maker/manufacturer - *seizosha* (say-ee-zoe-shah)
Men's department - *dansei yo* (dahn-say-ee yoe)

The men's department is on the 3rd floor
Dansei yo wa san gai ni arimasu
(Dahn-say-ee yoe wah sahn guy nee ah-ree-mahss)

Men's wear - *menzu wea* (men-zuu way-ah)
Open (for business) - *aite imasu* (aye-tay ee-mahss)
Open for business (sign) - *eigyo chu* (egg-yoe chuu)
Present/souvenir - *omiyage* (oh-me-yah-gay)
Receipt - *ryoshusho* (r'yoe-shuu-show); *reshito* (ray-shee-toe)

Here is your receipt
Ryoshusho de gozaimasu
(R'yoe-shuu-show day go-zie-mahss)

Return (a product) - *kaeshimasu* (kie-she-mahss)

Do you want to return that?
Sore wo *kaeshitai* desu ka?
(Soe-ray oh kie-she-tie dess kah?)

Sample - *mihon* (me-hoan)
Send - *okurimasu* (oh-kuu-ree-mahss)

Shall I send this to your home?

Kore wo o'uchi made okurimasho ka?
(Koe-ray oh oh-uu-chee mah-day oh-kuu-ree-mah-show kah?)

Service center - *sabisu senta* (sah-bee-sue sen-tah)
Ship (send) - *okurimasu* (oh-kuu-ree-mahss)
Shop (store) - *mise* (me-say)
Shopping - *kaimono* (kie-moe-no)
Shopping arcade - *shoppingu akedo* (shope-peen-guu ah-kay-doe)
Shopping bag - *shoppingu 6aggu* (shope-peen-guu bah-guu)
Shopping center - *shoppingu senta* (shope-peen-guu sen-tah)
Shopping mall - *shoppingu moru* (shope-peen-guu moe-rue);
meiten gai (may-ee-tane guy)

The nearest shopping mall is about 10 minutes from here
Ichiban chikai no shoppingu moru wa koko kara jippun gurai desu
(Ee-chee-bahn chee-kie no shope-peen-guu moe-rue wah koe-koe kah-rah jeep-poon guu-rye dess)

Shopping street - *shoten gai* (show-tane guy)

Size - *saizu* (sie-zoo)

Measurement - *sumpo* (sume-poe)

What is your collar size?
Kubi no saizu wa dono kurai desho ka?
(Kuu-bee no sie-zoo wah doe-no kuu-rye day-show kah?)

May I measure your waist size?
Weissuto no sumpo wo totte mo yoroshii desho ka?
(Way-ees-toe no sume-poe oh tote-tay moe yoe-roe-she-ee day-show kah?)

Sold out - *urikire* (uu-ree-kee-ray)

I'm sorry, but we're sold out
Sumimasen ga urikiremashita
(Sue-me-mah-sin gah uu-ree-kee-ray-mah-sshtah)

Sports wear - *supotsu wea* (spote-sue way-ah)
Supermarket - *supa* (sue-pah); *supa maketto* (sue-pah mah-ket-toe)
Take with you - *o'mochi kaerimasu* (oh-moe-chee kie-ree-mahss)

Underground shopping area/center - *chika gai* (chee-kah guy)
Women's department - *fujin yo* (fuu-jeen yoe)

The women's department is on the second floor
Fujin yo wa ni kai de gozaimasu
(Fuu-jeen yoe wah nee kie day go-zie-mahss)

Women's wear - *womenzu wea* (woe-men-zuu way-ah)
Wrap (in paper) - *tsutsumimasu* (t'sue-t'sue-me-mahss)
Wrapping paper - *hoso shi* (hoe-so she)

What kind of wrapping paper would you like?
Donna hoso shi wo hoshii desu ka?
(Doan-nah hoe-soe she oh hoe-she-ee dess kah?)

SHOPPING ITEMS

Bathing cap - *sui ebo* (sue-ee eh-boe)
Bathing suit - *kaisui gi* (kie-sue-ee ghee)
Bath robe - *basu robu* (bah-sue roe-buu); heya gi (hay-yah ghee)
Belt - *beruto* (bay-rue-toe)
Bikini *swimsuit* - *bikini* (be-kee-nee)
Blazer jacket - *bureza koto* (buu-ray-zah koe-toe)
Blouse - *burausu* (buu-rah-uu-sue)
Bolero tie - *borero* (boe-ray-roe)

Bow tie - *cho nekutai* (choe nay-kuu-tie)
Bra - *bura* (buu-rah)
Braces (suspenders) - *zubon-tsuri* (zoo-bone-t'sue-ree)
Buckle - *bakkuru* (bahk-kuu-rue)
Button - *botan* (boe-tahn)
Cap - *boshi* (boe-she)
Cardigan - *kadigan* (kah-dee-ghan)
Chiffon - *kinu mosurin* (kee-nuu moe-sue-reen)
Coat/jacket - *uwagi* (uu-wah-ghee)
Collar - *eri* (eh-ree); *kara* (kah-rah)
Corduory - *koruten* (koe-rue-tane)
Cotton - *momen* (moe-mane)
Cuffs - *kafusu* (kah-fuu-sue)
Dinner *jacket* (tux) - *takishido* (tah-kee-she-doe)
Dress - *doresu* (doe-ray-sue)
Dressing gown - *doreshingu gaon* (doe-ray-sheen-guu gown)
Dungarees - *dangarisu* (dahn-gah-ree-sue)
Dungaree trousers - *dangari zubon* (dahn-gah-ree zoo-bone)

Elastic - *gomu* (go-muu)
Evening dress - *ibuningu doresu* (ee-buu-neen-guu doe-ray-sue)
Felt - *feruto* (fay-rue-toe)
Flannel - *furano* (fuu-rah-no)
Gaberdine - *gyabajin* (g'yah-bah-jeen)
Girdle - *gadoru* (gah-doe-rue)
Gloves - *tebukuro* (tay-buu-kuu-roe)
Handkerchief - *hankachi* (hahn-kah-chee)
Hem - *fuchi* (fuu-chee)
Jacket - *jaketto* (jah-ket-toe)

Jeans - *jinzu* (jeen-zoo)
Jersey - *jaji* (jah-jee)
Jumper - *janpa* (jahn-pah)
Lace - *resu* (ray-sue)
Lapel - *raperu* (rah-pay-rue); *kaeshi-eri* (kie-she-eh-ree)
Leather - *kawa* (kah-wah)
Linen - *rinneru* (reen-nay-rue)
Lingerie - *shitagi* (she-tah-ghee)
Lining - *ura* (uu-rah)
Necktie - *nekutai* (nay-kuu-tie)
Nightdress (sleeping gown) - *nemaki* (nay-mah-kee)
Nylon - *nairon* (nie-roan)
Overcoat - *oba koto* (oh-bah koe-toe)
Personal check - *kojin kogitte* (koe-jeen koe-geet-tay)

Pique - *pike* (pee-kay)
Pocket - *poketto* (poe-ket-toe)
Poplin - *popurin* (poe-puu-reen)
Pullover - *puruoba* (puu-rue-oh-bah)
Pyjamas - *pajama* (pah-jah-mah)
Raincoat - *rein koto* (rain koe-toe)
Ribbon - *ribon* (ree-bone)
Rayon - *reyon* (ray-yoan)
Razor - *kamisori* (kah-me-soe-ree)
Razor blades - *kamisori no ha* (kah-me-soe-ree no hah)
Satin - *saten* (sah-tane)
Scarf- *sukafu* (sue-kah-fuu)
Serge - *saji* (sah-jee)
Shirt- *waishatsu* (wie-shah-t'sue)
Shoes - *kutsu* (koot-sue)
Short-sleeved shirt - *han-sode shatsu* (hahn-soe-day shah-t'sue)
Shorts - *shoto pantsu* (show-toe pahn-t'sue)
Silk- *kinu* (kee-nuu)
Skirt - *sukato* (sue-kah-toe)
Slacks - *surakkusu* (sue-rahk-sue)

Sleeve - *sode* (soe-day)
Slip - *surippu* (sue-reep-puu)
Slippers - *surippa* (sue-reep-pah)
Sneakers - *sunikka* (sue-neek-kah)
Socks, stockings - *kutsushita* (koot-sue-sshtah)
Sports jacket - *supotsu-yo* jaketto (sue-pote-sue yoe jah-ket-toe)
Suit (for men) - *sebiro* (say-be-roe); sutsu (sue-t'sue)
Suspenders - *zubontsuri* (zoo-bone-t'sue-ree)
Sweater - *seta* (say-tah)
Suede - *suedo gawa* (sway-doe gah-wah)
Suntan lotion/oil - *santan oiru* (sahn-tahn oh-ee-rue)
T-shirt - *T-shatsu* (tee-shaht-sue)
Tennis shoes - *tenisu gutsu* (tay-nee-sue goot-sue)
Toothpaste - *hamigaki* (hah-me-gah-kee)
Traveler's check - *torabera chekku* (toe-rah-bay-rah chek-kuu);
ryokosha kogitte (r'yoe-koe-shah koe-geet-tay)
Trousers - *zubon* (zoo-bone)
Tweed - *tsuido* (t'sue-ee-doe)
Velvet - *berubetto* (bay-rue-bet-toe); *birodo* (bee-roe-doe)
Wool - *uru* (uu-rue)
Worsted - usuteddo (uu-stay-doe)
Zipper - *jippa* (jeep-pah)

COLORS

Beige - *beju* (bay-juu)
Black - *kuro* (kuu-roe)
Blue - *buru* (buu-rue); ao (ah-oh)
Brown - *chairo* (chah-ee-roe)
Cream - *kurimu-iro* (kuu-ree-muu ee-roe)
Crimson - *shinkoshoku* (sheen-koe-show-kuu)
Emerald - *emurarudo gurin* (eh-muu-rah-rue-doe guu-reen)
Gold - *kiniro* (keen-ee-roe)
Green - *gurin* (guu-reen); *midori*-iro (mee-doe-ree-ee-roe)
Grey - *haiiro* (hi-ee-roe); *gurei* (guu-ray-ee)
Orange - *orenji* (oh-ren-jee)
Pink - *pinkku* (peen-kuu)
Purple - *murasaki-iro* (muu-rah-sah-kee-ee-roe)
Red - *akai* (ah-kie)
Silver - *gin-iro* (gheen-ee-roe)
Tan - *shibu-iro* (she-buu-ee-roe)
White - *shiro* (she-roe)
Yellow - *ki-iro* (kee-ee-roe)

CAMERA VOCABULARY

Black and white - *shiro kuro* (she-roe kuu-roe)
Cable release - *shatta rerisu* (shah-tah ray-ree-sue)
Camera - *kamera* (kah-may-rah)
Digital camera – *dejitaru kamera* (day-jee-tah-rue kah-may-rah)

Don't forget your camera!
Kamera wo wasurenai de!
(Kah-may-rah oh wah-sue-ray-nie day!)

Color film - *kara firumu* (kah-rah fee-rue-mue)
Develop - *genzo shimasu* (gane-zoe she-mahss)
Enlarge - *hikinobashimasu* (he-kee-no-bah-she-mahss)
Exposure counter - *firumu kaunta* (fee-rue-mue kah-uun-tah)
Exposure meter - *roshutsu ke* (roe-shute-sue kay)
Film - *firumu* (fee-rue-mue)

8 millimeter film - *hachi miri firumu* (hah-chee me-ree fee-rue-muu)
16 mm film - *juroku miri firumu* (juu-roe-kuu me-ree fee-rue-muu)
35 mm film - *sanjugo miri firumu* (sahn-juu-go me-ree fee-rue-muu)
20 exposures - *niju maki* (neejuu mah-kee)
36 exposures - *sanjuroku maki* (sahn-juu-roe-kuu mah-kee)

Flash bulbs - *furasshu barubu* (fuu-rahs-shuu bah-rue-buu)
Flash cubes - *furasshu kyubu* (fuu-rahs-shuu que-buu)
Filter - *firuta* (fee-rue-tah)

Red/yellow - *aka/kiiro* (ah-kah/kee-ee-roe)
Ultra violet - *shigai sen* (she-guy sen)
Lens - *renzu* (rane-zoo)
Lens cap - *renzu kyappu* (rane-zoo k'yahp-puu)
Lens cleaners - *renzu kurina* (rane-zoo kuu-ree-nah)
Negative - *nega* (nay-gah)
Processing charge - *genzo dai* (gane-zoe die)
Rangefinder - *renji fainda* (ranejee fine-dah)
Repair - *naoshimasu* (nah-oh-she-mahss)
Shutter - *shatta* (shah-tah)
Tripod - *sankyaku* (sahn-k'yah-kuu)

Zoom lens - *zumu renzu* (zoo-muu rane-zoo)

PART 7

THE SIGHTSEEING INDUSTRY

Key Words & Useful Sentences

Welcome! - *Irasshaimase!* (Ee-rah-shy-mah-say!)
Bus - *basu* (bah-sue)
Board (get on bus) - norimasu (no-ree-mahss)

Please board the bus
Basu ni notte kudasai
(Bah-sue nee note-tay kuu-dah-sie)

Camera - *kamera* (kah-may-rah)
Digital camera – *dejitaru kamera* (day-jee-tah-ruu kah-may-rah)

Do you have your camera(s)?
Kamera ga motte imasu ka?
(Kah-may-rah gah mote-tay ee-mahss kah?)

Color film - *karafirumu* (kah-rah fee-ruu-muu)
Color slide film - *kara suraidofirumu* (kah-rah sue-rie-doe fee-ruu-muu)

How about film?
Firumu wa?
(Fee-rue-muu wah?)

Develop (film) - *genzo shimasu* (ghen-zoe she-mahss)
Famous place(s) - *mei sho* (may-ee show)

There are many famous places in this area
Kono hen ni takusan mei sho ga arimasu
(Koe-no hane nee tock-sahn may-ee show gah ah-ree-mahss)

We are going to see a famous place
Mei sho wo mi ni ikimasu
(May-ee show oh me nee ee-kee-mahss)

Festival - *matsuri* (mot-sue-ree)

There will be a local festival here next week
Raishu koko de chihoteki no o'matsuri ga arimasu
(Rye-shuu koe-koe day chee-hoe-tay-kee no oh-mot-sue-ree gah

ah-ree-mahss)

Film - *firumu* (fee-ruu-muu)
Print - *purinto* (puu-reen-toe)

Guide - *annaisha* (ahn-nie-shah); *gaido* (guy-doe)

I am your guide
Watakushi wa annaisha desu
(Wah-tock-she wah ahn-nie-shah dess)
Yoroshiku onegaishimasu*
(Yoe-roe-she-kuu oh-nay-guy-she-mahss!)

*This is a very common institutionalized phrase used in any situation where the speaker wants the help, cooperation or understanding of the party being addressed. It has no precise English equivalent, but means something like "please help me, please cooperate, please be considerate," and so on. It is very Japanese, and very important in Japanese etiquette.

Guide book - *annai sho* (ahn-nie show); *gaido buku* (guy-doe buu-kuu)
Historical place - *kyu seki* (que say-kee)

This is a famous historical place
Kore wa yumei na kyu seki desu
(Koe-ray wah yuu-may-ee nah que say-kee dess)

Join (a tour) - *sanka* (sahn-kah)

Would you like to join a/the tour?
Tsuaa ni sanka shitai desu ka?
(T'sue-ah nee sahn-kah she-tie dess kah?)

It is a four-hour tour
Yoji-kan no tsuaa desu
(Yoe-jee-kahn no t'sue-ah dess)

The tour leaves at 8 a.m.
Tsuaa ga gozen no ha~hiji ni shuppatsu shimasu
(T'sue-ah gah go-zane no hah-chee-jee nee shupe-pot-sue she-mahss)
Full-day tour - hi-gaeri tsuaa (he-guy-ree t'sue-ah)

It is a full-day tour

Hi-gaeri tsuaa de gozaimasu
(He-guy-ree t'sue-ah day go-zie-mahss)

Kilometers - *kiro* (kee-roe)

Our destination is about 50 kilometers (from here)
Yukusaki wa daitai goju kiro desu
(Yuu-kuu-sah-kee wah die-tie go-juu kee-roe dess)

Photographs/pictures - *shashin* (shah-sheen)

Yes, you can take pictures
Hai, shashin toru koto ga dekimasu
(Hi, shah-sheen toe-rue koe-toe gah day-kee-mahss)

Pleasure trip - *go-manyu no ryoko* (go-mahn-yuu no r'yoe-koe)

Is this a pleasure trip?
Go-manyu no ryoko desu ka?
(Go-mahn-yuu no r'yoe-koe dess kah?)

Scenic beauty - *keshiki* (kay-she-kee)
Sightseer - *kanko-kyaku* (kahn-koe k'yah-kuu)
Sightseeing - *kanko* (kahn-koe); *kembutsu* (kem-boot-sue)
Sightseeing bus - *kanko basu* (kahn-koe bah-sue)
Sightseeing industry - *kanko sangyo* (kahn-koe sahn-g'yoe);
kembutsu sangyo (kem-boot-sue sahn-g'yoe)
Tour - *tsuaa* (t'sue-ah)
Tour price - *tsuaa no ryokin* (t'sue-ah no r'yoe-keen)

The tour bus starts here
Tsuaa no basu ga koko kara shuppatsu desu
(T'sue-ah no bah-sue gah koe-koe kah-rah shupe-pot-sue dess)

Travel agent - *kanko ryokosha* (kahn-koe r'yoe-koe-shah)

Admission charge - *nyujo ryo* (n'yuujoe r'yoe)

Some sightseeing attractions have admission charges
Aru kanko-butsu no tokoro wa nyujo ryo ga arimasu
(Ah-rue kahn-koe-boot-sue no toe-koe-roe wah n'yuujoe r'yoe
gah ah-ree-mahss)

Advance tickets - *maeuri no kippu* (my-uu-ree no keep-puu)

You should buy advance tickets

Maeuri no kippu wo kau ho ga ii desu
(My-uu-ree no keep-puu oh cow hoe ~ah ee dess)

Altitude - *takasa* (tah-kah-sah); *kodo* (koh-doe)

The altitude here is 2500 meters
Koko no takasa wa ni-sen-go-hyaku metoru desu
(Koe-koe no tah-kah-sah wah nee-sen-go-h'yah-kuu may-toe-rue dess)

Amusement park - *yu enchi* (yuu inn-chee)
Antiques - *kottohin* (kote-toe-heen)
Antique shop - *kotto ya* (kote-toe yah)

Would you like to go to an antique shop?
Kotto ya ni ikitai desu ka?
(Kote-toe yah nee ee-kee-tie dess kah?)

Aquarium - *suizokukan* (sue-ee-zoe-kuu-kahn)
Art - *geijutsu* (gay-ee-jute-sue)
Art gallery - *garo* (gah-roe)

There are many art galleries in Scottsdale
Sukotsuderu ni takusan garo ga arimasu
(Sue-kote-sue-day-rue nee tahk-sahn gah-roe gah ah-ree-mahss)

Barn - *naya* (nah-yah)
Beach - *biichi* (bee-chee); *kaigan* (kie-gahn)

Do you want to go to the beach?
Biichi ni ikitai desu ka?
(Bee-chee nee ee-kee-tie dess kah?)

Botanical garden - *shokubutsu en* (show-kuu-boot-sue in)
Bridge - *hashi* (hah-she); *buriji* (buu-ree-jee)
Brook (small stream of water) - *ogawa* (oh-gah-wah)
Building - biru (bee-rue); birudingu (bee-rue-deen-guu);
tatemono (tah-tay-moe-no)
Canal (large) - *unga* (uun-gah); small canal - *horiwari* (hoe-ree-wah-ree)
Castle - *shiro* (she-roe)
Cathedral - *daiseido* (die-say-ee-doe)
Cave - *iwaya* (ee-wah-yah)

There are many famous caves in America

Amerika ni takusan yumei na iwaya ga arimasu
(Ah-may-ree-kah nee tock-sahn yuu-may-ee nah ee-wah-ya gah
ah-ree-mahss)

Cemetery - *bochi* (boe-chee)
Ceremony - *gishiki* (ghee-she-kee)
Church - *kyokai* (k'yoe-kie)
Cliff - *gake* (gah-kay)
Cloudy - *kumotte imasu* (kuu-mote-tay ee-mahss)

Overcast - *ichimen ni kumotta* (ee-chee-mane nee kuu-mote-tah)

Cornfield - *mugibatake* (muu-ghee-bah-tah-kay)
Concert hall - *konsato horu* (kon-sah-toe hoe-rue)
Cottage - *koya* (koe-yah)
Countryside - *inaka* (ee-nah-kah)
Danger - *kiken* (kee-kane); *abunai* (ah-boo-nie)

It is dangerous here. Please be careful!
Koko wa abunai desu. Kiwotsukete kudasai!
(Koe-koe wah ah-buu-nie dess. Kee-oat-skay-tay kuu-dah-sie!)

Dock- *dokku* (doke-kuu)
Do not touch - *te wo furenaide kudasai* (tay oh fuu-ray-nie-day
kuu-dah-sie)
Downtown (area) - *shinai* (she-nie); *shitamachi* (ssh-tah-mah-
chee)
Elevation (above/below sea-level) - *kaibatsu* (kie-bot-sue)
Entrance fee - *nyujo ryo* (n'yuu-joe r'yoe)
Exhibition - *tenrankai* (tane-rahn-kie)
Factory- *kojo* (koe-joe)
Farm - *noka* (noh-kah)
Ferry - *feri* (fay-ree); *watashibune* (wah-tah-she-buu-nay)

We will cross the lake by ferry
Mizuumi wo feri de watarimasu
(Mee-zoo-uu-me oh fay-ree day wah-tah-ree-mahss)

Festival - *matsuri* (maht-sue-re); fesutibaru (fes-tee-bah-rue)

Yes, there are many local festivals in America
Hai, Amerika ni takusan chihoteki no matsuri ga arimasu
(Hi, Ah-may-ree-kah nee tahk-sahn chee-hoe-tay-kee no mot-
sue-ree gah ah-ree-mahss)

Field - *nohara* (no-hah-rah)

Fish market - *uo ichiba* (uu-oh ee-chee-bah)
Float (in a parade) - *dashi* (dah-she)
Folkcrafts - *mingeihin* (meen-gay-ee-heen)
Folk music - *minzoku ongaku* (meen-zoe-kuu own-gah-kuu)

Cowboy and country music is the folk music of America
Kaoboi to kantori no ongaku wa Amerika no minzoku ongaku desu
(Cowboy toe kahn-toe-ree no own-gah-kuu wah Ah-may-ree-kah no meen-zoe-kuu no own-gah-kuu dess)

Footpath - *yuhodo* (yuu-hoe-doe)
Forest - *mori* (moe-ree)
National forest - *kokuritsu mori* (koe-kuu-reet-sue moe-ree)

The world's largest forest of Ponderosa pine is in the state of Arizona
Sekai ju no ichiban okii na Ponderosa painu no mori wa Arizona shu ni arimasu
(Say-kie juu no ee-chee-bahn oh-kee-e nah Pon-day-roe-sah pie-nuu no moe-ree wah Ah-ree-zoe-nah shuu nee ah-ree-mahss)

Fountain - *izumi* (ee-zoo-me)
Gardens - *teien* (tay-ee-in); *gaaden* (gahh-dane)
Harbor/port - *minato* (me-nah-toe)
Hiking - *haikingu* (hi-keen-guu)
Go hiking - *haikingu ni ikimasu* (hi-keen-guu nee ee-kee-mahss)
Hill - *oka* (oh-kah)
House - *ie* (ee-eh)
Inn - *yadoya* (yah-doe-yah)*

*In the U.S. in particular, "inn" is sometimes synonymous with hotel, in which case it is better to use the word "inn" or "resort inn instead of the Japanese term yadoya, which implies a small, home-style lodging house.

Island - *shima* (she-mah); *jima* (jee-mah)

Hawaiian Islands - *Hawaii Shima* (Hah-wah-ee She-mah)
Guam Island - *Guwamu Shima* (Guu-wah-muu she-mah)

Lake - *mizuumi* (me-zoo-uu-me)
Library - *toshokan* (toe-show-kahn)

Lost and Found - *ishitsubutsu toriatsukaijo* (ee-she-t'sue-boot-sue toe-ree-aht-sue-kie-joe)
Marsh - *numachi* (nuu-mah-chee)
Memorial (monument) - *kinenhi* (kee-nane-he)
Monument (ancient/historical/scenic) - *shiteki kinembutsu* (she-tay-kee kee-name-boot-sue) Mountain - *yama* (yah-mah); also *san* (sahn) when used in compounds
Mountain dimbing - *yama nobori* (yah-mah no-boe-ree)
Mountain peak - *mine* (me-nay)
Mountain range - *san myaku* (sahn m'yah-kuu)
Movie house - *eiga kan* (eh-ee-gah kahn)
Museum (historical) - *hakubutsukan* (hah-kuu-boot-sue-kahn)

Archeological museum - *kohko kan* (koeh-koe kahn)
Fine arts museum - *bijutsu kan* (beejute-sue kahn)
Science museum - *kagaku-hakubutsu kan* (kah-gah-kuu-hahkuu-boot-sue kan)

National treasures - *koku ho* (koe-kuu hoe)
No Parking (sign) - *chusha kinshi* (chuu-shah keen-she)

Parking is now allowed here
Koko de chusha wo kinshi shite imasu
(Koe-koe day chuu-shah oh keen-she ssh-tay ee-mahss)

No photo-taking - *satsuei kinshi* (saht-sue-eh-ee keen-she)
No smoking - *kin'en* (keen-inn)
Observatory - *tenmondai* (tane-moan-die)
Off-limits - *tachiiri-kinshi* (tah-chee-ee-ree keen-she)
Opera house - *opera za* (oh-pay-rah zah)
Painting - *kaiga* (kie-gah)
Palace - *paresu* (pah-ray-sue); *kyuden* (que-dane)
Park - koen (koe-in)
National park- *kokuritsu koen* (koe-kuu-reet-sue koe-in)
Parking place (for cars) - chusha jo (chuu-shah joe)

The parking lot is behind the hotel
Chusha jo wa hoteru no ura ni arimasu
(Chuu-shah joe wah hoe-tay-rue no uu-rah nee ah-ree-mahss)

Path - *komichi* (koe-me-chee)
Peak - *mine* (me-nay)
Peninsula - *hanto* (hahn-toe)
Planetarium - *puranetariumu* (puu-rah-nay-tah-ree-uu-muu)
Plantation - noen (noh-in)
Pond - *ike* (ee-kay)

Pool - *puru* (puu-rue)
Pottery - *togei* (toh-gay-ee)
Rain - *ame* (ah-may)

It is starting to rain
Ame ga furi dashimashita
(Ah-may gah fuu-ree dah-she-mah-sshta)

Rainy season - *nyu bai* (n'yuu by)

Our rainy season starts next month
Watakushi-tachi no nyu bai wa raigetsu hajimarimasu
(Wah-tock-she-tah-chee no n'yuu by wah rye-gate-sue hah-jee-mah-ree-mahss)

River - *kawa* (kah-wah); *gawa* (gah-wah)
Road - *michi* (me-chee)

This road goes to _____
Kono michi wa _____ e ikimasu
(Koe-no mee-chee wah _____ eh ee-kee-mahss)

Rock - *iwa* (ee-wah); rocky place - *iwa no oi tokoro* (ee-wah no oh-ee toe-koe-roe)
Ruins - *iseki* (ee-say-kee)
Sea/ocean - *umi* (uu-me)

Seashore - *kaigan* (kie-gahn)
Seasickness - *funayoi* (fuu-nah-yoe-ee)

Are you seasick?
Funayoi shite imasu ka?
(Fuu-nah-yoe-ee ssh-tay ee-mahss kah?)

Sculpture - *chokoku* (choe-koe-kuu)
Shopping center - *shoppingu senta* (shope-peen-guu sen-tah)
Spring (water) - *mizuba* (mee-zoo-bah)
Stream - *ogawa* (oh-gah-wah)
Stadium - *kyogijo* (k'yoe-ghee-joe); *sutajiamu* (stah-jee-ahm)
Statue - *zo* (zoe)
Stroll (walk) - *sampo* (sahm-poe)

Have a nice walk
Yoi sampo wo shite kudasai
(Yoe-ee sahm-poe oh ssh-tay kuu-dah-sie)

Swamp - *shitchi* (sheet-chee)
Synagogue - *yudaya kyokai* (yuu-dah-yah k'yoe-kie)
Theater (stage) - *gekijo* (gay-kee-joe)
Toilet (washroom) - *otearai* (oh-tay-ah-rye)
Tower - *taoa* (tah-oh-ah); *to* (toe)
Tree - ki (kee)
Evergreen tree - *tokiwa gi* (toe-kee-wah ghee)
University- *daigaku* (die-gah-kuu)
Valley - *tani* (tah-nee)
Village - *mura* (muu-rah)
Vineyard - *budoen* (buu-doe-in)
Walk (stroll) - *sampo* (sahm-poe)
Waterfall - *taki* (tah-kee)

The most famous waterfall in America is in Niagara, New York
Amerika no ichi6an yumei na taki wa Naiagara, Nyu Yoku ni arimasu
(Ah-may-ree-kah no ee-chee-bahn yuu-may-ee nah tah-kee wah
Nie-ahgah-rah,
N'yuu Yoe-kuu nee ah-ree-mahss)

Water fountain - *fun sui* (foon sue-ee)
Watermill - *suisha* (suu-ee-shah)
Weather - *o'tenki* (oh-tane-kee)
Well (for water) - *ido* (ee-doe)
Wildlife - *yasei-seibutsu* (yah-say-ee-say-ee-boot-sue)
Zoo - *dobutsuen* (doe-boot-sue-in)

PART 8

THE ENTERTAINMENT AND RECREATION INDUSTRIES

Key Words & Useful Sentences

Entertainment - *goraku* (go-rah-kuu); *kantai* (kahn-tie); *yokyo* (yoe-k'yoe)
Recreation - *kibarashi* (kee-bah-rah-she); *rekurieshon* (ree-kuu-ree-ayshone)
Actor(s) - *haiyu* (hie-yuu)
Actress(es) - *joyu* (joe-yuu)
Adventure story - *boken mono* (boe-kane moe-no)
Adult - *otona* (oh-toe-nah)

Adult ticket - *otona no kippu* (oh-toe-nah no keep-puu)

How many tickets do you need?
Kippu ga nan mai irimasu ka?
(Keep-puu gah nahn my ee-ree-mahss kah?)

Advance ticket sales - *mae uri kippu* (my uu-ree keep-puu)
Amusing, entertaining - *omoshiroi* (oh-moe-she-roy)

I heard that the movie is very interesting
Sono eiga wa taihen omoshiroi to kikimashita
(So-no eh-ee-gah wah tie-hane oh-moe-she-roy toe kee-kee-mah-sshtah)

Applause - *hakushu-kassai* (hock-shuu kahs-sie)
Applaud (cheer) - *hakushu kassai shimasu* (hock-shuu kahs-sie she-mahss)
Ballet - *bare* (bah-ray)

Do you like ballet?
Bare wo suki desu ka?
(Bah-ray oh skee dess kah?)

Bilingual - *nika-kokugo* (nee-kah-koe-kuu-go)

I believe the movie is bilingual
Sono eiga ga nika-kokugo to omoimasu
(So-no eh-ee-gah gah nee-kah-koe-kuu-go toe oh-moy-ee-mahss)

Box office - *kippu uriba* (keep-puu uu-ree-bah)
Broadcast - *hoso* (hoe-so)
Child's ticket - kodomo no kippu (koe-doe-moe no keep-puu)
Comedy - kigeki (kee-gay-kee)

Concert - *ongakukai* (own-gah-kuu-kie); *konsato* (kone-sah-toe)

The concert begins at 8 P.M.
Konsato wa yoru no hachiji ni hajimarimasu
(Kone-sah-toe wah yoe-rue no hah-cheejee nee hahjee-mah-re-mahss)

Cover charge - *kaba chaji* (kah-bah chah-jee)
Seat/cover charge - *seki ryo* (say-kee r'yoe)
Crime story - *hanzai mono* (hahn-zie moe-no)
Director - *kantoku* (kahn-toe-kuu)

Drama (play) - engeki (in-gay-kee); *dorama* (doe-rah-mah)
Musical drama - *ongaku geki* (own-gah-kuu gay-kee)
Historical drama - shi geki (she gay-kee)
Dubbed (in some language) - *fukikae* (fuu-kee-kie)

No, the movie is not dubbed
Iie, sono eiga wa fukikae de wa arimasen
(Ee-eh, so-no eh-ee-gah wah fuu-kee-kie day wah ah-ree-mah-sin)

Enjoy- *tanoshimimasu* (tah-no-she-me-mahss)
Enjoyable - *tanoshii* (tah-no-she-ee)

Enjoy the game
Gemu wo tanoshimi kudasai
(Gay-muu oh tah-no-she-me kuu-dah-sie)

Entrance - *iriguchi* (ee-ree-guu-chee)
Evening dress - *yakai fuku* (yah-kie fuu-kuu); *ibuningu doresu*
(ee-buu-neen-guu do-ray-sue)

An evening dress is required
Ibuningu doresu ga hitsuyo desu
(Ee-buu-neen-guu doe-ray-sue gah he-t'sue-yoe dess)

Exit - *deguchi* (day-guu-chee)
Folk dance - minzoku buyo (meen-zoe-kuu buu-yoe)
Full - *manseki* (mahn-say-kee)

The theater is full
Gekijo wa manseki desu
(Gay-kee-joe wah mahn-say-kee dess)

General admission seats - *ippan seki* (eep-pahn say-kee)

There are still some general admission seats
Mada ippan seki ga arimasu
(Mah-dah eep-pahn say-kee gah ah-ree-mahss)

Horror film - *kyofu eiga* (k'yoe-fuu eh-ee-gah)
Jazz - *jazu* (jah-zoo)
Love story - *renai mono* (rain-aye moe-no)
Movie - *eiga* (eh-ee-gah)
Movie theater - *eiga kan* (eh-ee-gah kahn)

There are several movie theaters near here

Kono chikaku ni su eiga kan ga arimasu
(Koe-no chee-kah-kuu nee sue eh-ee-gah kahn gah ah-ree-mahss)

Movie star - *haiyu* (hi-yuu)
Music - *ongaku* (own-gah-kuu)
Musical concert - *ongaku kai* (own-gah-kuu kie)

There is a musical concert tonight
Komban ongaku kai ga arimasu
(Kome-bahn own-gah-kuu kie gah ah-ree-mahss)

Shall I get tickets for you?
Kippu wo torimasho ka?
(Keep-puu oh toe-ree-mah-show kah?)

Mystery - *suirimono* (sue-ee-ree-moe-no)
Now showing (film) - *joei chu* (joe-eh-ee chuu)

Today's (feature) - *to jitsu* (toe jeet-sue)

Now showing (theatrical play) - *joen chu* (joe-inn chuu)
Opening time - *kaijo jikan* (kiejoe jee-kahn)

Opening time is 8 o'clock
Kaijo jikan wa hachiji desu
(Kiejoe jee-kahn wah hah-cheejee dess)

Opera - *opera* (oh-pay-rah)
Opera glasses - opera gurasu (oh-pay-rah guu-rah-sue)
Performance - *bu* (buu)
Play (fare) - *geki* (gay-kee)
Playguide - *purei gaido* (puu-ray-ee guy-doe)

Popular (good repuation) - *hyoban ga ii* (h'yoe-bahn gah ee);
ninki ga arimasu (neen-kee gah ah-ree-mahss)

That movie is very popular
Sono eiga wa taihen ninki ga arimasu
(So-no eh-ee-gah wah tie-hane neen-kee gah ah-ree-mahss)

Program - *puroguramu* (puu-roe-guu-rah-muu)
Reservations - *yoyaku* (yoe-yah-kuu)
Reserved seat - *shitei seki* (she-tay-ee say-kee)
Roadshow (first-run) - *rodo sho* (roe-doe show)
Rock and roll - *rokku ando roru* (roke-kuu ahn-doe roe-rue)

Seat - *seki* (say-kee)
Showing/playing - *joei saremasu* (joe-eh-ee sah-ray-mahss)

This movie is showing until tomorrow
Kono eiga wa ashita made joei sarete imasu
(Koe-no eh-ee-gah wah ah-ssh-tah mah-day joe-eh-ee sah-ray-
tay ee-mahss)

Standing room - *tachi mi* (tah-chee me)
Standing room only - *tachi mi dake* (tah-chee me dah-kay)

I'm sorry, now there is standing room only
Sumimasen ga, ima wa tachi mi dake desu
(Sue-me-mah-sin gah, ee-mah wah tah-chee me dah-kay dess)

Star (of movie) - *shuyaku* (shuu-yah-kuu)
Starting time - *hajimaru jikan* (hah-jee-mah-rue jee-kahn);
kaien jikan (kie-in jee-kahn)
Student - *gakusei* (gahk-say-ee)

Are you a student?
Anata wa gakusei desu ka?
(Ah-nah-tah wah gahk-say-ee dess kah?)

If you are a student, the tickets are cheaper
Gakusei deshitara kippu ga motto yasui desu
(Gahk-say-ee desh-tah-rah keep-puu gah mote-toe yah-sue-ee
dess)

Subtitled - *ji-maku* (jee-mah-kuu)

Yes, the movie has subtitles
Hai, sono eiga wa ji-maku ga arimasu
(Hi, so-no eh-ee-gah wah jee-mah-kuu gah ah-ree-mahss)

Theater - *gekijo* (gay-kee-joe); *shieta* (she-ay-tah)
Ticket - *kippu* (keep-puu); *nyujo-ken* (n'yuu-joe ken)
Ticket(s) for today's show - *tojitsu ken* (toe-jeet-sue ken)

We are now selling tickets for today's show
Ima tojitsu ken wo utte imasu
(Ee-mah toe-jeet-sue ken oh uut-tay ee-mahss)

Ticket(s) for future showing - *maeuri ken* (my-uu-ree ken)

We will start selling tickets for future showings at 4 P.M.

Gogo yoji ni maeuri ken wo uri hajimarimasu
(Go-go yoe-jee nee my-uu-ree ken oh uu-ree hah-jee-mah-ree-mahss)

Unreserved seat - *jiyu seki* (jee-yuu say-kee)
Western (film) - *seibu geki* (say-ee-buu gay-kee)

Today's film is a Western
Tojitsu no eiga wa seibu geki desu
(Toe-jeet-sue no eh-ee-gah wah say-ee-buu gay-kee dess)

BARS, CABARETS AND NIGHTCLUBS

Bar - *ba* (bah)
Cabaret - *kyabare* (k'yah-bah-ray)
Lounge - *raunji* (rah-uun-jee)
Nightclub - *naito kurabu* (nie-toe kuu-rah-buu)
Dance (Western style) - *dansu* (dahn-sue); to dance - *odorimasu* (oh-doeree-mahss)

There is a dance tonight
Komban dansu ga arimasu
(Kome-bahn dahn-sue gah ah-ree-mahss)

Do you like to dance?
Dansu wo suki desu ka?
(Dahn-sue oh skee dess kah?)

Floor show - *furoa sho* (fuu-roe-ah show)

The next floor show will be at 11 o'clock
Tsugi no furoa sho wa ju-ichi ji desu
(T'sue-ghee no fuu-roe-ah show wah juu-ee-chee jee dess)

Hostess (in cabaret/nightclub) - *hosutesu* (hoe-sue-tay-sue)

We do not have Japanese-style hostesses
Nihon sutairu no hosutesu wa imasen
(Nee-hoan sue-tie-rue no hoe-sue-tay-sue wah ee-mah-sin)

Live show - *raibu sho* (rye-buu show)

There are two live shows every night
Mai ban nikai no raibu sho ga arimasu
(My bahn nee-kie no rye-buu show gah ah-ree-mahss)

Sing - *uta wo utaimasu* (uu-tah oh uu-tie-mahss)
Singer - *kashu* (kah-shuu); *uta o utau hito* (uu-tah oh uu-tah-uu ssh-toe)

I hear that singing is a national pastime in Japan
Nihon ni wa uta ga kokuritsu no tanoshimi da so desu
(Nee-hoan nee wah uu-tah gah koe-kuu-reet-sue no tah-no-she-me dah so dess)

Do you sing?
Anata wa uta wo utai ni narimasu ka?
(Ah-nah-tah wah uu-tah oh uu-tie nee nah-ree-mahss kah?)

He/she sings very well
Anohito wa uta ga jozu desu
(Ah-no-ssh-toe wah uu-tah gah joe-zoo dess)

But I am really awful (at singing)
Shikashi, watakushi wa honto ni heta desu
(She-kah-shi wah-tock-she wah hoan-toe nee hay-tah dess)

Vocalist - *seigaku-ka* (say-ee-gah-kuu-kah)

SPORTS VOCBULARY

Athlete(s) - *undoka* (uun-doe-kah)
Athletic meet - *kyogi kai* (k'yoe-ghee kie)
Athletics - *undokyogi* (uun-doe-k'yoe-ghee)
Boxer - *kentoka* (ken-toe-kah); *bokusa* (boke-sah)
Boxing - *kento* (ken-toe); *bokushingu* (boke-sheen-guu)

Are you interested in boxing?
Kento ni kiyomi ga arimasu ka?
(Ken-toe nee k'yoe-me gah ah-ree-mahss kah?)

There is a boxing match tonight
Komban kento shiai ga arimasu
(Kome-bahn ken-toe she-aye gah ah-ree-mahss)

Champion (defending) - *yogosha* (yoe-go-shah)
Championship (victory) - *yusho* (yuu-show)
Coach - *kochi* (koe-chee)
Trainer - *torena* (toe-ray-nah)
Exercise - *undo* (uun-doe)

What do you do for exercise?
Undo no tame ni nani wo shimasu ka?
(Uun-doe no tah-me nee nah-nee oh she-mahss kah?)

Facilities - *shisetsu* (she-sate-sue)
Game (sporting contest) - *kyogi* (k'yoe-ghee); game for
amusement - *yugi* (yuu-ghee); *gemu* (gay-muu)
Lose (match/game) - *makemasu* (mah-kay-mahss)

The champion lost
Yogosha wa makemashita
(Yoe-go-shah wa mah-kay-mah-sshtah)

Match - *shiai* (she-aye)
Opposing team – *taisen aite* (tie-sen aye-tay)
Play (a sport) – yugi (yuu-ghee); *supotsu suru* (sue-poe-t'sue
sue-rue)
Play for amusement - *asobimasu* (ah-soe-bee-mahss)

What kind of amusement do you like?
Donna asobi wo suki desu ka?
(Doan-nah ah-so-bee oh skee dess kah?)

Player - *senshu* (sane-shuu); *pureya* (puu-ray-yah)
Playground - *undoba* (uun-doe-bah)
Recreation - *kisanji* (kee-sahn-jee); *rekurieshon* (re-kuu-ree-ay-
shone)
Referee - *refuri* (ray-ruu-ree)
Rival - *aite* (aye-tay); *kyoso aite* (k'yoe-soe aye-tay); *raibaru*
(rye-bah-rue)
Score - *tokutensu* (toe-kuu-tane-sue); *sukoa* (sue-koe-ah)

The score is now 3 to 7
Ima no sukoa wa san tai nana desu
(Ee-mah no sue-koe-ah wah sahn tie nah-nah dess)

Sports - *undo* (uun-doe);*supotsu* (spoe-t'sue)
Indoor sports - *okunai undo* (oh-kuu-nie uun-doe); *okunai
supotsu* (ohkuu-nie spoe-t'sue)
Out door sports – *kogai supotsu* (koe-guy spoe-t'sue)

What kind of sports do you play?
Donna supotsu wo oyari ni narimasu ka?
(Doan-nah spoe-t'sue oh oh-yah-ree nee nah-ree-mahss kah?)

Starting time - *hajimaru jikan* (hah-jee-mah-rue jee-kahn)
Win - *kachimasu* (kah-chee-mahss)

The champion won
Yogosha wa kachimashita
(Yoe-go-shah wah kah-chee-mah-sshtah)

Winner - *yushosha* (yuu-show-shah)
Win the championship - *yusho shimasu* (yuu-show she-mahss)
Win a race - *resu ni kachimasu* (ray-sue nee kah-chee-mahss)
Victory - *shori* (show-ree); *yusho* (yuu-show)
Celebrate a victory - *shori wo iwaimasu* (show-ree oh ee-wie-mahss)

Let's celebrate
O'iwai shimasho
(Oh-ee-wie she-mah-show)

BASEBALL

Back net - *bakku netto* (bahk-kuu net-toe)
Back screen - *bakku sukuriin* (bahk-kuu skuu-reen)
Ball (as in balls and strikes) - *boru* (boe-rue)
Baseball - *yakyu* (yah-que); *besu boru* (bay-sue boe-rue)
Baseball diamond - *besuboru daiyamondo* (bay-sue boe-rue die-yah-moan-doe)
Baseball game/match - *yakyu shiai* (yah-que she-aye)
Bases 1st base - *ichirui* (ee-chee-rue-ee)
2nd base - *nirui* (nee-rue-ee)
3rd base - *sanrui* (sahn-rue-ee)
Bases loaded - *furu besu* (fuu-rue bay-sue); *manrui* (mahn-rue-ee)
Base men first base man - *fasuto* (fahs-toe) second base man - *sekando* (say-kahn-doe) third base man - *sado* (sah-doe) short-stop - *shoto* (show-toe)
Bat - *batto* (baht-toe)
Batter - *batta* (bat-tah)
Batter's box - *batta bokkusu* (baht-tah boke-kuu-sue)
Batting stance - *battingu sutansu* (baht-teen-guu sue-tahn-sue)
Block sign - *buroku sain* (buu-roe-kuu sign)
Bunt - *banto* (bahn-toe)

Catcher - *kyatcha* (k'yah-chah)
Change-up (pitch) - *chenji appu* (chain-jee ahp-puu)
Cheerleader - *chiarida* (chee-ah-ree-dah)

Coach - *kochi* (Koe-chee)
Cut-off play - *chukei pure* (chuu-kay-ee puu-ray-ee)
Day game - *de gemu* (day gay-muu)
Dead ball - *deddo boru* (ded-doe boe-rue)
Double-header - *daburu hedda* (dah-buu-rue heh-dah)
Doubleplay - *daburu pure* (dah-buu-rue puu-ray); *gettsu* (gett-t'sue) or "get two
Error - *era* (eh-rah) Extra innings - *encho sen* (inn-choe sen)
Farm club - *famu* (fah-muu); *nigun* (nee-goon)
Fielder(s) - *firuda* (fee-rue-dah)
Center fielder - *senta* (sen-tah) left fielder - *refuto* (ref-toe) right fielder - *raito* (rye-toe)
Foul ball - *fauru* (fah-uu-rue)
Full count - *furu kaunto* (fue-rue koun-toe)
Grand-slam home run - *manrui homa* (mahn-rue-ee hoe-mah)
Grounder - *goro* (go-roe)
Helmet - *herumetto* (hay-rue-met-toe)
Hit - *hitto* (heet-toe)
Inning - *kai* (kie); *iningu* (ee-neen-guu)

1st inning - dai ikkai (die eek-kie)
2nd inning - dai nikai (die nee-kie)
3rd inning - dai sankai (die sahn-kie)
4th inning - dai yonkai (die yoan-kie)
5th inning - dai gokai (die go-kie)
6th inning - dai rokkai (die roke-kie)
7th inning - dai nanakai (die nah-nah-kie)
8th inning - dai hachikai (die hah-chee-kie)
9th inning - dai kyukai (die que-kie)

Top (of an inning) - *omote* (oh-moe-tay)*
Bottom (of an inning) - *ura* (uu-rah)*

*In Japanese innings are divided into "front" (*omote*) and "back" (*ura*) instead of top and bottom.

Line drive - *raina* (rye-nah)
Lose (a game/match) - *makemasu* (mah-kay-mahss)
Manager - *kantoku* (kahn-toe-kuu); *maneja* (mah-nay-jah)
Out - *auto* (ow-toe)
Over-time - *oba taimu* (oh-bah tie-muu)
Pinch hitter - *pinchi hitta* (peen-chee heet-tah)
Pinch runner - *pinchi rana* (peen-chee rah-nah)
Pitcher - *pitcha* (peet-chah)
Pitching mound - *maundo* (moun-doe)
Runner crossing the plate (scoring a run) - *homuin* (hoe-mu-

een)
Sacrifice bunt - *gisei banto* (ghee-say-ee bahn-toe)
Sacrifice fly - *gisei furai* (ghee-say-ee fuu-rye)
Score - *sukoa* (sue-koe-ah)
Scoreboard - s*ukoabodo* (sue-koe-ah-boe-doe)
Straight fastball - sutoreto (steo-ray-toe)
Strike - *sutoraiki* (sue-toe-rye-kee); *sutoraiku* (sue-toe-rye-kuu)
Switch-hitter - *suichi hitta* (sue-we-chee heet-tah)
Tie game - *doro gemu* (doe-roe gay-muu)
Touch-out, tag-out - *tatchi auto* (tah-chee ow-toe)
Umpire - *ampaiya* (ahm-pie-yah)

BOATING AND SAILING

Canoe - *kanu* (kah-nuu)
Motorboat - *motaboto* (moe-tah-boe-toe)
Rowboat - *boto* (boe-tow)
Sailboat - *hokake bune* (hoe-kah-kay buu-nay)

To raise the sail - *ho wo agemasu* (hoe oh ah-gay-mahss)
To lower the sail - *ho wo oroshimasu* (hoe oh oh-roe-she-mahss)

All right! All together! Raise the sail!
Sa! Issho ni! Ho wo agenasai!
(Sah! Ees-show nee! Hoe oh ah-gay-nah-sie!)

Yacht - yatto (yaht-toe)
Deck chair - *dekki chea* (day-kee chay-ah)

Would you like a deck-chair?
Dekki chea wa ikaga desho ka?
(Day-kee chay-ah wah ee-kah-gah dess kah?)

Hourly charge - *ichi-jikan no ryokin* (ee-cheejee-kahn no r'yoe-keen)

The hourly charge is dollars
Ichi-jikan no ryokin wa doru desu
(Ee-chee-jee-kahn no r'yoe-keen wah doe-rue dess)

Rent - *karimasu* (kah-ree-mahss)

Would you like to rent a boat?

Boto wo karitai desu ka?
(Boe-tow oh kah-ree-tie dess kah?)

Race - *kyoso* (k'yoe-soe); *resu* (ray-sue)
Boat race - *boto resu* (boe-toe ray-sue)

BOWLING

Bowling - *boringu* (boe-reen-guu)

Bowling is very popular here. Would you like to try it?
Koko de boringu wa taihen ninki ga arimasu. Yatte mitai desu ka?
(Koe-koe day boe-reen-guu wah tie-hane neen-kee gah ah-ree-mahss.
Yaht-tay me-tie dess kah?)

CAMPING

Camping - *kyampingu* (k'yahm-peen-guu)

Have you been camping before?
Mae ni kyampingu shita koto ga arimasu ka?
(My nee k'yahmp-peen-guu sshtah koe-toe gah ah-ree-mahss kah?)

Campgrounds - *kyampu jo* (k'yahm-puu joe)
Official campgrounds - *konin no kyampu jo* (koe-neen no k'yahm-puu joe)

If you want to stay at official campgrounds, you must make reservations
Moshi, konin no kyampu jo ni tomaritai nara yoyaku wo tora nakereba narimasen
(Moe-she, koe-neen no k'yahm-puu joe nee toe-mah-ree-tie nah-rah yoe-yah-kuu oh
toe-rah nah-kay-ray-bay nah-ree-mah-sin)

Drinking water - *inryo sui* (een-r'yoe sue-ee); *nomi mizu* (no-me me-zoo)

No, it doesn't have drinking water
Iie, nomi mizu ga arimasen
(Ee-eh, no-me me-zoo gah ah-ree-mah-sin)

Showers - *shawa* (shah-wah)

Toilet - *toire* (toe-ee-ray)
Washroom - *tearai* (tay-ah-rye)
Shop - *baiten* (by-tane)

We can provide you with all of the necessary equipment
Hitsuyo na setsubi wo zembu yoi suru koto ga dekimasu
(He-t'sue-yoe nah say-t'sue-bee oh zim-buu yoe-ee sue-rue koe-
toe gah day-kee-mahss)

FISHING

Bait - *beito* (bay-ee-toe)
Fish - *sakana* (sah-kah-nah); uo (uu-oh)
Fishing - *tsuri* (t'sue-ree)

Go fishing - *tsuri ni ikimasu* (t'sue-ree nee ee-kee-mahss)

Who wants to go fishing?
Donata ga tsuri ni ikitai desu ka?
(Doe-nah-tah gah t'sue-ree nee ee-kee-tie dess kah?)

If you would like to go fishing, please make reservations
Tsuri ni ikitai nara, yoyaku wo shite kudasai
(T'sue-ree nee ee-kee-tie nah-rah, yoe-yah-kuu oh ssh-tay kuu-
dah-sie)

Fishing gear - *fishingu gia* (fee-sheen-guu ghee-ah)
Fishing rod - *tsuri zao* (t'sue-ree zah-oh); *roddo* (rode-doe)
Fishing line - *tsuri ito* (t'sue-ree ee-toe); *rain* (rine)
Fishing tackle - *tsuri dogu* (t'sue-ree doe-guu); *takkuru* (tahk-
kuu-rue)
Fish net - *tsuri ami* (t'sue-ree ah-me)
Fly - *furai* (fuu-rye)
Hook- *hukku* (huuk-kuu)
Lure - *rua* (rue-ah)
Reel - *riru* (ree-rue)
Sinker - *waki* (wah-kee); *sinka* (seen-kah)
Spool - *supuru* (sue-puu-rue)

Boat - *boto* (boe-toe)
Lake - *ike* (ee-kay)
Ocean - *umi* (uu-me)

River - *kawa* (kah-wah)

GOLF

Golf – *gorufu* (go-ruu-fuu)
Arnateur - *amachua* (ah-mah-chuu-ah); shiroto (she-roe-toe)
Bag - *baggu* (bahg-gu)
Ball - *boru* (boe-rue)
Birdie - *badei* (bah-day-ee)
Blind hole - *buraindo horu* (buu-rine-doe hoe-rue)
Bogie - *bogi* (boe-ghee)
Caddy - *kyadi* (k'yah-dee)
Club - *kurabu* (kuu-rah-buu)
Clubhouse - *kurabu hausu* (kuu-rah-buu hah-uu-sue)
Course - *kosu* (koe-sue)
Driving range - *doraibingu renji* (doe-rye-been-guu ranejee)
Driver - *doraiba* (doe-rye-bah)
Eagle - *igaru* (ee-gah-rue)
Fairway - *feawei* (fay-ah-way)
Golf- *gorufu* (go-rue-fuu)

Do you play golf?
Gorufu wo nasaimasu ka?
(Go-rue-fuu oh nah-sie-mahss kah?)

Golf clubs - *gorufu kurabu* (go-rue-fuu kuu-rah-buu)
Golf course - *gorufu jo* (go-rue-fuu joe)
Golfer - *gorufa* (go-rue-fah)
Golfing - *gorufingu* (go-rue-feen-guu)
Grass - *shibafu* (she-bah-fuu)
Green - *gurin* (guu-reen)
Grip - *gurippu* (guu-reep-puu)
Group - *gurupu* (guu-rue-puu)

How many are there in your group?
Anato no gurupu ni nan mei sama de gozaimasu ka?
(Ah-nah-tah no guu-rue-puu nee nahn may-ee sah-mah day go-
zie-mahss kah?)

Holes - *horu* (hoe-rue)
Iron - *airon* (aye-roan)
Lesson - *ressun* (rays-soon)
Lie - *rai* (rye)
Pin - *pin* (peen)
Pro - *puro* (puu-roe)
Putter - *patta* (pah-tah)

Putting - *pattingu* (pah-teen-guu)
Rough - *rafu* (rah-fuu)
Sand - *suna* (sue-nah)
Score - *sukoa* (sue-koe-ah)
Shoes - *shuzu* (shuu-zoo)
Shaft - *shafuto* (shah-fuu-toe)
Slice - *suraisu* (sue-rye-sue)
Straight- *sutoreto* (straigh-toe)
Stroke - *sutoroku* (stro-kuu)
Swing - *suwingu* (sue-ween-guu)
Tee - *ti* (tee) Tee off- *ti ofu* (tee oh-fuu)
Water - *mizu* (me-zoo)
Wood - *uddo* (uud-doe)
Yard - *yado* (yah-doe)

Shall I make reservations for you?
Yoyaku wo torimasho ka?
(Yoe-yah-kuu oh toe-ree-mah-show kah?)

HORSE RACING

Horse - *uma* (uu-mah)
Horse race - kei ba (kay-ee bah)

Would you like to see a horse race?
Kei ba wo mitai desu ka?)
(Kay-ee bah oh me-tie dess kah?)

Race track (for horse-racing) - *kei-ba jo* (kay-ee-bah joe)
Bet (wager) - *kake* (kah-kay)
Bet on a horse/the horses - *uma ni kakemasu* (uu-mah nee kah-kay-mahss)
Make money on a horse race - *kei ba de mokeru* (kay-ee bah day moe-kay-rue)
Lose money on a horse race - *kei ba de son suru* (kay-ee bah day soan sue-rue)
Hit a dark horse/long shot - *ana wo ateru* (ah-nah oh ah-tay-rue)*

*By itself the Japanese word *ana* means "hole, slit, gap."

SKATING / SKIING

Skate - *suketo* (skay-toe)

Rental skates - *kariru suketo* (kah-ree-rue skay-toe)
Skate shoes - *suketo gutsu* (skay-toe goot-sue)
Skating rink- *suketo jo* (skay-toe joe)

Can you skate?
Suketo ga dekimasu ka?
(Skay-toe gah day-kee-mahss kah?)

Ski - *suki* (skee); skiing - *suki* (skee)

Do you like to ski?
Suki ga suki desu ka?
(Skee gah skee dess kah?)

Ski resort (place) - *suki jo* (skee joe)
Ski equipment - *suki dogu* (skee doe-guu)
Ski boots - *suki butsu* (skee buu-t'sue)
Rent - *karimasu* (kah-ree-mahss)
Rental boots - *kariru butsu* (kah-ree-rue buu-t'sue)
Rental skis - *kariru ski* (kah-ree-rue skee)
Ski conditions - *suki joken* (skee joe-kane)

I hear the ski conditions today are very good
Kyo no suki joken ga totemo ii so desu
(K'yoe no skee joe-kane ga toe-tay-moe ee soh dess)

Ski lessons - *suki ressun* (skee res-soon); *suki keiko* (skee kay-ee-koe)
Charge for lessons - *ressun ryo* (res-soon r'yoe)

The one-hour lesson charge is _____ dollars
Ichiji kan no ressun ryo wa _____ doru desu
(Ee-chee-jee-kahn no res-soon r'yoe wah ____ doe-rue dess)

Ski lift - *suki rifuto* (skee reef-toe)
Charge for ski lift - *suki rifuto ryo* (skee reef-toe r'yoe)

SWIMMING AT THE BEACH

Beach - *bichi* (bee-chee); *kaigan* (kie-gahn)

Are you going to the beach tomorrow?
Ashita bichi ni ikimasu ka?
(Ah-sshtah bee-chee nee ee-kee-mahss kah?)

Big waves - *onami* (oh-nah-me)
Calm (water) - *odayaka* (oh-dah-yah-kah)
Dangerous- *kiken* (kee-kane)

Be careful. The high waves are dangerous
Kiwotsukete. Onami wa kiken desu
(Kee-oat-skay-tay. Oh-nah-me wah kee-kane dess)

Deep - *fukai* (fuu-kie)

It gets deep very quickly
Sugu fukaku ni narimasu
(Sue-guu fuu-kah-kuu nee nah-ree-mahss)

Depth - *fukasa* (fuu-kah-sah)
High tide - *mancho* (mahn-choe)
Lifeguard - *miharinin* (me-hah-ree-neen)
Low tide - *kancho* (kahn-choe)
Rocky beach - *iwaba no bichi* (ee-wah-bah no bee-chee)
Sandy beach - *sunahama no bichi* (suu-nah-hah-mah no bee-chee)
Shallow - *asai* (ah-sie)

Don't worry. It's very shallow
Shimpai naku. Taihen asai desu
(Sheem-pie nah-kuu. Tie-hane ah-sie dess)

Swim - *oyogu* (oh-yoe-guu)
Swimmer - *oyogite* (oh-yoe-ghee-tay)
Swimming - *oyogi* (oh-yoe-ghee)

Can you swim?
Oyogu koto ga dekimasu ka?
(Oh-yoe-guu koe-toe gah day-kee-mahss kah?)

Swimming pool - *puru* (puu-rue)

Indoor pool - *okunai puru* (oh-kuu-nie puu-rue)
Outside pool - *okugai puru* (oh-kuu-guy puu-rue)
Heated pool - *danbo shite iru puru* (dahn-boe ssh-tay ee-rue puu-rue)

Surf- *safu* (sah-fuu)
Surfboard - *safingu bodo* (sah-feen-guu boe-doe)
Towel - *taoru* (tah-oh-rue)
Waves - *nami* (nah-me)

Water skis - *suijo suki* (suu-ee-joe skee)
Water temperature - *sui on* (suu-ee own)

The water is cold today
Kyo wa mizu ga tsumetai desu
(K'yoe wah me-zoo gah t'sue-may-tie dess)

But the air is warm
Shikashi, kuki ga atatakai desu
(She-kah-she, kuu-kee gah ah-tah-tah-kie dess)

TENN I S

Tennis - *tenisu* (tay-nee-sue)
Tennis ball - *tenisu boru* (tay-nee-sue boe-rue)
Tennis club - *tenisu kurabu* (tay-nee-sue kuu-rah-buu)
Tennis court - *tenisu koto* (tay-nee-sue koe-toe)
Tennis match - *tenisu shiai* (tay-nee-sue she-aye)
Tennis net - *tenisu no ami* (tay-nee-sue no ah-me); netto (net-toe)
Tennis racket - *tenisu raketto* (tay-nee-sue rah-ket-toe)

Do you play tennis?
Tenisu wo nasaimasu ka?
(Tay-nee-sue oh nah-sie-mahss kah?)

Would you like to play today?
Kyo oyari ni narimasu ka?
(K'yoe oh-yah-ree nee nah-ree-mahss kah?)

I will reserve a court for you
Koto wo yoyaku shimasu
(Koe-toe oh yoe-yah-kuu she-mahss)

What time would you like to start?
Nanji ni hajimaritai desu ka?
(Nahnjee nee hah-jee-mah-ree-tie dess kah?)

Advantage - *adobanteji* (ah-doe-bahn-tay-jee)
Approach - *apuroehi* (ah-puu-roe-chee)
Backhand - *bakkuhando* (bahk-kuu-hahn-doe)
Balance - *baransu* (bah-rahn-sue)
Ball - *boru* (boe-rue)
Club - *kurabu* (kuu-rah-buu)
Coach - *kochi* (koe-chee)

Couple - *kapuru* (kah-puu-rue)
Court - *koto* (koe-toe)
Doubles - *daburusu* (dah-buu-rue-sue)
Forehand - *foahando* (foe-ah-hahn-doe)
Racket - *raketto* (rah-ket-toe)
Rental - *rentaru* (ren-tah-rue)
Rules - *ruru* (rue-rue)
Serve - *sabu* (sah-buu)
Service - *sabisu* (sah-bee-sue)
Shoes - *shuzu* (shuu-zoo)
Singles - *shingaru* (sheen-gah-rue)
Tennis clinic - *tenisu kurinkku* (tay-nee-sue kuu-ree-neek-kuu)

PART 9

THE TRAVEL AGENCY BUSINESS

Key Words & Useful Sentences

Welcome! - *Irasshaimase!* (Ee-rah-shy-mah-say!)
Travel, traveling - *ryoko* (r'yoe-koe)
Traveler - *ryokosha* (r'yoe-koe-shah)
Travel agent - *ryoko dairiten* (r'yoe-koe die-ree-tane)

Are you the only one (traveling)?
O'hitori desu ka
(Oh-ssh-toe-ree dess kah?)

Where do you wish to go?
Doko e ikitai no desu ka?
(Doe-koe eh ee-kee-tie no dess kah?)

How many days do you wish to stay?
Nan nichi ni taizai shitai desu ka?
(Nahn nee-chee nee tie-zie she-tie dess kah?)

Business travel - *shoyo ryoko* (show-yoe r'yoe-koe)
Pleasure travel - *manyu ryoko* (mahn-yuu r'yoe-koe)

Is this a pleasure trip?
Kore wa manyu no ryoko desu ka?
(Koe-ray wah mahn-yuu no r'yoe-koe dess kah?)

Airline - *koku gaisha* (koe-kuu guy-shah)

Which airline do you prefer?
Dochira no koku gaisha no ho ga ii desho ka?
(Doe-chee-rah no koe-kuu guy-shah no hoe gah ee day-show kah?)

Reservations - *yoyaku* (yoe-yah-kuu)

I have confirmed your reservations
Yoyaku wo kakunin shimashita
(Yoe-yah-kuu oh kah-kuu-neen she-mah-sshtah)

Your ticket is ready
Kippu wo yoi shite arimasu
(Keep-puu oh yoe-ee ssh-tay ah-ree-mahss)

Will you be picking up your ticket today?
Kyo kippu wo tori ni kuru desho ka?
(K'yoe keep-puu oh toe-ree nee kuu-rue day-show kah?)

First-class - *fasuto kurasu* (fahss-toe kuu-rah-suu)
Business dass - *bijinesu kurasu* (bejee-nay-sue kuu-rah-sue)
Economy class - *ekonomi kurasu* (eh-koe-no-me ku-rah-sue)
Credit card - *kurejitto kaado* (kuu-ray-jeet-toe kah-doe)

Will you be paying by credit card?
Kurejitto kaado de o'shiharai desu ka?
(Kuu-rayjeet-toe kah-doe day oh-she-hah-rye dess kah?)

Aisle seat - *tsurogawa no o'zaseki* (t'sue-roe-gah-wah no oh-zah-say-kee)

Do you prefer an aisle seat?
Tsurogawa no o'zaseki no ho ga ii desu ka?
(T'sue-roe-gah-wah no oh-zah-say-kee no hoe gah ee dess kah?)

Middle seat - *mannaka no o'zaseki* (mahn-nah-kah no oh-zah-say-kee)
Window seat - *madogawa no ozaseki* (mah-doe-gah-wah no oh-zah-say-kee)
Passport - *pasupoto* (pahss-poe-toe)
Visa - *bisa* (bee-sah)
Boarding pass - *tojoken* (toejoe-ken)

This is your boarding pass

Kore wa tojoken desu
(Koe-ray wah toe-joe-ken dess)

Connections - *noritsugi* (no-ree-t'sue-ghee)
Stopover - *tochugesha* (toe-chuu-gay-shah)

There is a two-hour stopover in Dallas
Darasu de nijikan no tochugesha ga arimasu
(Dah-rah-sue day neejee-kahn no toe-chuu-gay-shah gah ah-ree-mahss)

Connecting flight - *noritsugi bin* (no-ree-t'sue-ghee bean)

Your connecting flight leaves from Gate10
Noritsugi bin wah ju geito kara demasu
(No-ree-t'sue-ghee bean wah juu gay-ee-toe kah-rah day-mahss)

Departure date - *shuppatsu no hizuke* (shupe-pot-sue no he-zoo-kay)

You leave on January 16
Ichigatsu no juroku nichi ni tachimasu
(Ee-chee-got-sue no juu-roe-kuu nee-chee nee tah-chee-mahss)

You arrive in Tokyo on the following day
Sono tsugi no hi ni Tokyo e tsukimasu
(So-no t'sue-ghee no he nee Tokyo eh t'sue-kee-mahss)

Departure time - *shuppatsu jikan* (shupe-pot-sue jee-kahn)

Your departure time is 12:30 P.M.
Shuppatsu jikan wa juniji han desu
(Shupe-pot-sue jee-kahn wah juu-nee-jee hahn dess)

Arrival date - *tochaku no hizuke* (toe-chah-kuu no he-zoo-kay)

You arrive on January 17
Tochaku no hizuke wa Ichigatsu no jushichi nichi desu
(Toe-chah-kuu no he-zoo-kay wah Ee-chee-got-sue no juu-she-chee nee-chee dess)

Arrival time - *tochaku jikan* (toe-chah-kuu jee-kahn)

Your arrival time is 3:30 P.M.
Tochaku jikan wa gogo no sanji han desu
(Toe-chah-kuu jee-kahn wah go-go no sahn-jee hahn dess)

Hotel - *hoteru* (hoe-tay-rue)

Do you have a preference in hotels?
Hoteru to shite sentaku ga arimasu ka?
(Hoe-tay-rue toe sshtay sane-tah-kuu gah ah-ree-mahss kah?)

Hotel reservations - *hoteru no yoyaku* (hoe-tay-rue no yoe-yah-kuu)

Your hotel reservations have been confirmed
Hoteru no yoyaku wa kakuritsu shimashita
(Hoe-tay-rue no yoe-yah-kuu wah kah-kuu-ree-t'sue she-mah-sshtah)

Your confirmation number is written down here
Kakunin bango wa koko ni kaite arimasu
(Kah-kuu-neen bahn-go wah koe-koe nee kie-tay ah-ree-mahss)

Rental car - *renta ka* (ren-tah kah)

Do you want/need a rental car?
Renta ka ga irimasu ka?
(Ren-tah kah gah ee-ree-mahss kah?)

Do you have an international driver's license?
Kokusai unten menkyo ga aru desho ka?
(Koke-sie uun-tane mane-k'yoe gah ah-rue day-show kah?)

Tour - *tsuaa* (t'sue-ah)
Tour group - *tsuaa gurupu* (t'sue-ah guu-rue-puu)
Ship - *fune* (huu-nay)*

*This word may be prounounced as *fuu-nay* or *huu-nay*, but the "h" sound is more common.

Passenger ship - *kyaku sen* (k'yah-kuu sen) Steamship - kisen (kee-sen)

Board a ship - *josen suru* (joe-sen sue-rue)

You may go aboard anytime after 2 P.M.
Gogo no niji kara nanji demo josen dekimasu
(Go-go no nee-jee kah-rah nahn-jee day-moe joe-sen day-kee-mahss)

Sailing date - *shuppatsu hizuke* (shupe-pot-sue he-zoo-kay)

The ship's sailing date is October 2
Fune no shuppatsu hizuke wa jugatsu no ni nichi desu
(Huu-nay no shupe-pot-sue he-zoo-kay wah juu-got-sue no nee
nee-chee dess)

Sailing time - *shuppatsu jikan* (shupe-pot-sue jee-kahn)

The ship's sailing time is 6 P.M.
Fune no shuppatsu jikan wa rokuji desu
(Fuu-nay no shupe-pot-sue jee-kahn wah roe-kuu-jee dess)

Pier - *sambashi* (sahm-bah-she)

Your ship leaves from Pier 7
Anata no fune wa Sambashi Nanaban kara demasu
(Ah-nah-tah no fuu-nay wah Sahm-bah-she Nah-nah-bahn kah-
rah day-mahss)

Port - minato (me-nah-toe)
Port of destination - tochaku ko (toe-chah-kuu koe)
Seasick - funayoi (fuu-nah-yoe-e)

Do you get seasick?
Funayoi wo nasaimasu ka?
(Fuu-nah-yoe-ee oh nah-sie-mahss kah?)

PART 10

FOR THE HOME-VISIT HOST

Key Words & Useful Sentences

Home (our, my) - *uchi* (uu-chee); your home - *o'uchi* (oh-uu-
chee)

Welcome to our home
Uchi ni yoku irasshaimashita
(Uu-chee nee yoe-kuu ee-rah-shy-mah-sshta)

Please come in
Dozo, o-hairi kudasai
(Doe-zoe, oh-hie-ree kuu-dah-sie)

My name is (I am) _____
Watakushi wa _____   *desu*
(Wah-tock-she wah _____   dess)

I'm pleased to meet you
Hajimemashite, dozo yoroshiku
(Hah-jee-may-mah-sshtay, doe-zoe yoe-roe-she-kuu)

May I take your coat?
Koto wo azukari shimasho ka?
(Koe-toe oh ah-zoo-kah-ree she-mah-show kah?)

Husband (the speaker's spouse) - *shujin* (shuu-jeen)
Husband (the other party's spouse) - *go-shujin* (go-shuu-jeen)
Wife (the speaker's spouse) - *kanai* (kah-nie)
Wife (the other party's wife) - *okusan* (oak-sahn)

This is my husband, Tom
Konohito wa shujin no "Tomn desu
(Koe-no-ssh-toe wah shuu-jeen no "Tom" dess)

This is my wife, Sue
Konohito wa kanai no "Sue" desu
(Koe-no-ssh-toe wah kah-nie no "Sue" dess)

Children - *kodomo* (koe-doe-moe); *o'ko san* (oh-koe sahn)*

*When asking if someone else has children it is common to use the more polite (honorific) o'ko san (oh-koe sahn).

These are our children
Konohito tachi wa uchi no kodomo desu
(Koe-no-ssh-toe tah-chee wah uu-chee no koe-doe-moe dess)

Daughter (my, our) - *musume* (muu-sue-may)
Daughter (the other person's) – *o'josan* (oh-joe-sahn)
Son - *musuko* (muu-sue-koe)
Baby - *akanbo* (ah-kahn-boe); *aka chan* (ah-kah chan)

This is our daughter, Sheri
Konohito wa musume no "Sheri" desu
(Koe-no-ssh-toe wah muu-sue-may no "Sheri" dess)

This is our son, Michael

Konohito wa musuko no "Michael" desu
(Koe-no-ssh-toe wah muu-sue-koe no "Michael" dess)

_____ is the oldest
_____ *wa ichiban ue desu*
(_____ wah ee-chee-bahn way dess)

_____ is the youngest
_____ *wa ichiban shita desu*
(_____ wah ee-chee-bahn ssh-tah dess)

_____ is our first son/daughter
_____ *wa ue no musuko/musume desu*
(_____ wah way no muu-sue-koe/muu-sue-may dess)

This is our second son/daughter
Konohito wa nibamme no musuko/musume desu
(Koe-no-ssh-toe wah nee-bahm-may no muu-sue-koe/muu-sue-may dess)

This is our third son/daughter
Konohito wa sanbamme no musuko/musume desu
(Koe-no-ssh-toe wah sahn-bahm-may no muu-sue-koe/muu-sue-may dess)

Please sit down
Dozo, okake kudasai
(Doe-zoe oh-kah-kay kuu-dah-sie)

Please make yourself comfortable (be at ease)
Dozo, raku ni shite kudasai
(Doe-zoe, rah-kuu nee ssh-tay kuu-dah-sie)

Name - *namae* (nah-my)
Age - *toshi* (toe-she)
Kindergarten - *yochien* (yoe-chee-inn)
School - *gakko* (gahk-koe)
Elementary school - *sho gakko* (show gahk-koe)
High school - *koto gakko* (koe-toe gahk-koe)
College/university - *daigaku* (die-gah-kuu)

Our oldest daughter graduated from the university last year
Ue no musume ga kyonen daigaku kara sotsugyo shimashita
(Way no muu-sue-may gah k'yoe-nane die-gah-kuu kah-rah so-t'sue-g'yoe she-mah-sshtah)

Our second daughter is a senior in high school
Nibamme no musume wa koto gakko no yon nen sei desu
(Nee-bahm-may no muu-sue-may wah yoan nane say-ee dess)
Marriage - kekkon (keck-kone)

We have been married for 23 years
Nijusan nen ni kekkon shite imashita
(Nee-juu-sahn nane nee keck-kone sshtay ee-mah-sshtah)

Honeymoon - *shinkon* (sheen-kone)
Honeymoon trip - *shinkon ryoko* (sheen-kone r'yoe-koe)
Family - *kazoku* (kah-zoe-kuu)
Daughter-in-law - *yome* (yoe-may)
Son-in-law - *muko* (muu-koe)

This is our son-in-law, Mark
Konohito wa muko no "Mark" desu
(Koe-no-ssh-toe wah muu-koe no "Mark" dess)

Mother - *okasan* (oh-kah-sahn)
Father - *otosan* (oh-toe-sahn)
Father-in-law - *shuto* (shuu-toe)
Mother-in-law - *shutome* (shuu-toe-may)

This is my mother-in-law, Ruby
Konohito wa shutome no "Rubyn desu
(Koe-no-ssh-toe wah shuu-toe-may no "Ruby" dess)

Work- *shigoto* (she-goe-toe)
House work - *uchi no shigoto* (uu-chee no she-go-toe)
Part-time work - *arubaito* (ah-rue-by-toe)

I work part-time
Arubaito shite imasu
(Ah-rue-by-toe ssh-tay ee-mahss)

May I offer you a drink?
O-nomimono way ikaga desu ka?
(Oh-no-me-moe-no wah ee-kah-gah dess kah?)

What kind of Western food do you like?
Yoshoku to shite nani ga suki desu ka?
(Yoe-show-kuu toe ssh-tay nah-nee gah skee dess kah?)

Breakfast/lunch/dinner is served (done/ready).
Please (come to the table and be seated).

Gohan wa dekimashita. Dozo.
(Go-hahn wah day-kee-mah-sshtah. Doe-zoe.)

Please do not stand on ceremony. Help yourself.
Go enryo naku. Go-ju ni totte kudasai.
(Go inn-r'yoe nah-kuu. Go juu nee tote-tay kuu-dah-sie.)

Can you eat a little more?
Mo sukoshi taberare masu ka?
(Moe sue-koe-she tah-bay-rah-ray mahss kah?)

Would like to have dessert?
Dezato wa ikaga desu ka?
(Day-zah-toe wa ee-kah-gah dess kah?)

Chocolate ice cream - *chokoreto aisu kurimu* (choe-koe-ray-toe
aye-sue kuu-ree-muu)
Vanilla ice cream - *banira aisu kurimu* (bah-nee-rah aye-sue
kuu-ree-muu)
Strawberry ice cream - *sutoroberi aisu kurimu* (suu-toe-roe-bay-
ree aye-sue kuu-ree-muu)
Apple pie - *apuru pai* (ahp-puu-rue pie)
Banana cream pie - *banana kurimu pai* (bah-nah-nah kuu-ree-
muu pie)
Pumpkin pie - *pampukin pai* (pahm-puu-keen pie)
Chocolate cake - *chokoreto keki* (choe-koe-ray-toe kay-kee)
Carrot cake - *kyarotto keki* (k'yah-rote-toe kay-kee)
Fruit - *furutsu* (fuu-rute-sue)
Wash room - *O'tearai* (oh-tay-ah-rye)

The washroom is the second door on the right
O'tearai wa migi gawa no ni bamme no doa desu
(Oh-tay-ah-rye wah me-ghee gah-wah no nee bahm-may no
doe-ah dess)

I/we will take you to the airport
Hikojo made okutte agemasu
(He-koe-joe mah-day oh-kute-tay ah-gay-mahss)

We really enjoyed your visit
Homon shita koto wa hijo ni tanoshikata desu
(Hoe-moan ssh-tah koe-toe wah he-joe nee tah-no-she-kah-tah
dess)

Please come again

Mata irasshite kudasai
(Mah-tah ee-rah-ssh-tay kuu-dah-sie)

Please give this to your children
Kodomo san ni kore wo agete kudasai
(Koe-doe-moe sahn nee koe-ray oh ah-gay-tay kuu-dah-sie)

This is for your wife (husband)
Kore wa oku sama (danna sama) no tame desu
(Koe-ray wah oak sah-mah (dahn-nah sah-mah) no tah-may dess)

Please take care of yourself
Dozo, odaiji ni
(Doe-zoe, oh-die-jee nee)

Goodby
Sayonara
(Sah-yoe-nah-rah)

PART 11

ACCIDENTS AND ILLNESSES

Key Words & Useful Sentences

Accident - *jiko* (jee-koe)

You have been in a serious accident
Judai jiko ni aimashita
(Juu-die jee-koe nee aye-mah-sshtah)

I have called for help
Tetsudai wo yobimashita
(Tate-sue-die oh yoe-bee-mah-sshtah)

Acute - *kyusei* (que-say-ee)
Ambulance - *kyukyusha* (que-que-shah)
Asthma - *zensoku* (zen-soe-kuu)
At ease/relaxed - *anshin* (ahn-sheen)

Please rest easy/don't excite yourself
Anshin shite kudasai
(Ahn-sheen sshtay kuu-dah-sie)

Bandage - *hotai* (hoe-tie)
Body temperature - 36.5 degrees Centigrade (normal) - *roku-do gobu* (roe-kuu-doe go-buu)
Call - *yobimasu* (yoe-be-mahss)

I have called an ambulance
Kyukyusha wo yobimashita
(Que-que-shah oh yoe-bee-mah-sshtah)

Consulting room - *shinsatsu shitsu* (sheen-saht-sue sheet-sue)
Crutches - *matsubazue* (maht-sue-bah-zoo-eh)
Dentist - *haisha* (hah-ee-shah)

If it hurts, please tell me
Itamimashitara oshiete kudasai
(Ee-tah-me-mahssh-tah-rah oh-she-eh-tay kuu-dah-sie)

Doctor - *isha* (ee-shah); *O'isha* san (Oh-ee-shah sahn)*

*The "o" and "san" are honorific, but are so commonly used that they are more like essential parts of the word for doctor.

Shall I call a doctor?
O'isha san wo yobimasho ka?
(Oh-ee-sha sahn oh yoe-bee-mah-show kah?)

Drugstore - *kusuriya* (kuu-sue-ree-yah)

There is a drugstore just two or three minutes from here
Koko kara ni sanpun de kusuriya ga arimasu
(Koe-koe kah-rah nee sahn-poon day kuu-sue-ree-yah gah ah-ree-mahss)

Ear Nose Throat Department - *Ji Bi Inko Ka* (jee bee een-koe kah)
Emergency - *kyukan* (que-kahn)
Eye(s) - *me* (may)
Eye drops - *me gusuri* (may guu-sue-ree)
Eyeglasses - *megane* (may-gah-nay)
Food poisoning - *shokuchu-doku* (show-kuu-chuu-doe-kuu)
Help - *tetsudaimasu* (tay-t'sue-die-mahss)

May I help you?
O'tetsudai itashimasho ka?
(Oh-tay-t'sue-die ee-tah-she-mah-show kah?)

Hospital - *byoin* (b'yoe-een)
Reception counter/desk/window - *uketsuke* (uu-kay-t'sue-kay)
Be hospitalized - *nyuin shimasu* (n'yuu-een she-mahss)
Be discharged - *tai-in shimasu* (tie-een she-mahss)

I will take you to the hospital
Byoin e tsurete agemasu
(Be-yoe-een eh t'sue-ray-tay ah-gay-mahss)

Hurt - *itai* (ee-tie); to hurt - *itamimasu* (ee-tah-me-mahss)

Did you hurt your arm?
Ude ni kega wo shimashita ka?
(Uu-day nee kay-gah oh she-mah-sshta kah?)

Does it hurt?
Itai de gozaimasu ka?
(Ee-tie day go-zie-mahss kah?)

Injury - *kega* (kay-gah)

Have you been (were you) injured?
Kega wo shimashita ka?
(Kay-gah oh she-mah-sshtah kah?)

In-patient - *nyu-in* (n'yuu-een)
Internal Medicine Department - *nai ka* (nie kah)
Medical examination - *shin satsu* (sheen saht-sue)

I must give you a medical examination
Shin satsu wo shinakereba narimasen
(Sheen saht-sue oh she-nah-kay-ray-bah nah-ree-mah-sin)

Medicine - *kusuri* (kuu-sue-ree)

Take (liquid or pill) medicine - *kusuri wo nomimasu* (kuu-sue-ree oh no-me-mahss)

Please take this medicine
Kono kusuri wo nonde kudasai
(Koe-no kuu-sue-ree oh noan-day kuu-dah-sie)

Nasal spray - *tenki yaku* (tane-kee yah-kuu)
Nurse - *kangofu* (kahn-go-fuu)
Obstetrics and Gynecology Department - *san fujin ka* (sahn fuu-

jeen kah)
Office hours - *shinsatsu jikan* (sheen-saht-sue jee-kahn)
Ointment - *nanko* (nahn-koe)
Operation - *shujutsu* (shuu-jute-sue)
Ophthalmic Department - *gan ka* (gahn kah)
Out-patient - *tai-in* (tie-een)
Patient - *kanja* (kahn-jah)
Pediatrics Department - *shoni ka* (show-nee kah)
Prescription - *shoho* (show-hoe); prescription slip/form - *shoho sen* (show-hoe sen)

Do you have a prescription?
Shoho sen o'mochi de gozaimasu ka?
(Show-hoe sen oh-moe-chee day go-zie-mahss kah?)

Rest - *yasumi* (yah-sue-me)

You must rest
Yasuma nakereba narimasen
(Yah-sue-mah nah-kay-ray-bah nah-ree-mah-sin)

Sick - *byoki* (b'yoe-kee); *kagen ga warui* (kah-gane gah wah-rue-e)

Do you feel sick?
Go-byoki de gozaimasu ka?
(Go-b'yoe-kee day go-zie-mahss kah?)

Surgery Department - *ge ka* (gay kah)

Faint - *kizetsu shimasu* (kee-zay-t'sue she-mahss)
Fever- *netsu* (nate-sue)

You have a high fever. It is better for you to stay in bed
Netsu ga takai no de, neru ho ga ii desu
(Nay-t'sue gah tah-kie no day, nay-rue hoh ga ee dess)

Filling (tooth) - *tsumemono* (t'sue-may-moe-no)
Finger - *yubi* (yuu-bee)
First-aid kit - *kyukyu bako* (que-que bah-koe)
Foot - *ashi* (ah-she)
Forehead - *hitai* (he-tie)
Gargle - *ugai wo shimasu* (uu-guy oh she-mahss)
Gauze - *gaze* (gah-zay)
Hand - *te* (tay)
Hangover - *fiutsukayoi* (fuuts-kah-yoe-ee)

Head - *atama* (ah-tah-mah)
Headache - *atama ga itai* (ah-tah-mah ga ee-tie)

Medicine for headache - *zutsu yaku* (zuut-sue yah-kuu)

Heart - *shinzo* (sheen-zoe)
Heart attack - *shinzo mahi* (sheen-zoe mah-hee)
Heel - *kakato* (kah-kah-toe)
Hemorrhoids - *ji* (jee)
Hip - *shiri* (she-ree)
Hives - *jinmashin* (jeen-mah-sheen)
Indigestion - *shokafuryo* (show-kah-fuu-r'yoe)
Injection - *chusha* (chuu-shah)
Insect bites - *mushi sasare* (muu-she sah-sah-ray)
Intestines - *cho* (choh)
Itch - *kayui* (kah-yuu-ee)
Medicine for itch - *kayumi dome* (kah-yuu-me doe-may)

Kidney - *jinzo* (jeen-zoe)
Knee - *hiza* (he-zah)
Laxative - *gezai* (gay-zie)
Leg - *ashi* (ah-she)
Lie down - *yoko ni suru* (yoe-koe nee sue-rue)
Liver - *kanzo* (kahn-zoe)
Medicine - *kusuri* (kuu-sue-ree)
Mouth - *kuchi* (kuu-chee)
Muscle - *kinniku* (keen-nee-kuu)
Nail - *tsume* (t'sue-may)
Nail clippers - *tsume kiri* (t'sue-may kee-ree)
Nauseous - *hakike ga shimasu* (hah-kee-kay gah she-mahss)
Neck - *kubi* (kuu-bee)
Nerves - *shinkei* (sheen-kay-ee)
Nose - *hana* (hah-nah)
Nosebleed - *hanaji wo dashimasu* (hah-nah-jee oh dah-she-mahss)
Operation - *shujutsu* (shuu-jute-sue)
Patient - *kanja* (kahn-jah)
Physical examination - *kenko shindan* (kane-koe sheen-dahn)
Pill, tablet - *ganyaku* (gahn-yah-kuu)
One tablet - *ichi jo* (ee-chee joe)
Plaster - *bansoku* (bahn-soe-kuu)
Poison, poisonous - *doku* (doe-kuu)
Prescription - *shohosen* (show-hoe-sen)
Pulse - *myaku* (m'yah-kuu)
Rash - hasshin (hahs-sheen)
Rib - *rokkotsu* (roke-kote-sue)

Runny nose - *hana no mizu ga demasu* (hah-nah no mee-zoo gah day-mahss)
Sanitary napkin - *seiryo napukin* (say-ee-r'yoe nahp-keen)
Sedative - *chinseizai* (cheen-say-ee-zie)
Shoulder - *kata* (kah-tah)
Skin - *hifu* (he-fuu)
Sleep - *nemasu* (nay-mahss)
Sneeze - *kushami wo shimasu* (kuu-shah-me oh she-mahss)
Sole of foot - *tsumasaki* (t'sue-mah-sah-kee)
Spine - *sebone* (say-boe-nay)
Sprain - *nenza* (nane-zah)
Sting - *sasarekizu* (sah-sah-ray-kee-zoo)
Stomach - *i* (ee); *onaka* (oh-nah-kah)
Stomachache - *onaka ga itai* (oh-nah-kah ga ee-tie)
Stomach medicine - *i gusuri* (ee guu-sue-ree)
Swelling - *haremono* (hah-ray-moe-no)
Tablet - *ganyaku* (gahn-yah-kuu); *jo* (joe)
Thermometer - *taionkei* (tie-own-kay-ee)
Thigh - *momo* (moe-moe)
Throat - *nodo* (no-doe)
Thumb - *oyayubi* (oh-yah-yuu-be)
Thumb pressure (massage) - *shi atsu* (she aht-sue)
Toe - *ashinoyubi* (ah-she-no-yuu-be)
Tongue - *shita* (ssh-tah)
Tonsils - *hentosen* (hane-toe-sen)
Tonsilitis - *hentosen'en* (hane-toe-sen-inn)
Tooth - *ha* (hah)
Toothache - *ha ga itai* (hah gah ee-tie)

Front - *mae* (my)
Back - *ura* (uu-rah)
Top - *ue* (way)
Bottom - *shita* (ssh-tah)

Upset stomach - *onaka no guwai ga warui* (on-nah-kah no guu-wah-ee gah wah-rue-ee)
Urine - *shoben* (show-bane)
Urinate - *shoben suru* (show-bane sue-rue)
Venereal disease - *sei byo* (say-ee b'yoe)
Vitamins - *bitamin* (bee-tah-meen);
Vitamin pills - *bitamin zai* (bee-tah-meen zie)
Vomit - *haku shimasu* (hah-kuu she-mahss)
Womb - *shikyu* (she-que)
Wrist - *tekubi* (tay-kuu-be)
X-ray - *rentogen* (ren-toe-gane); X-ray (X-su ray)

MEDICAL DIRECTIONS
1 pill at a time - *ikkai ichi jo* (eek-kie ee-chee joe)
2 pills at a time - *ikkai ni jo* (eek-kie nee joe)
1 capsule at a time - *ikkai ni kapuseru ikko* (eek-kie nee kah-puu-say-rue eek-koe)
2 capsules at a time - *ikkai ni kapurseru niko* (eek-kie nee kah-puu-say-rue nee-koe)
After meals - *shoku go ni* (show-kuu go nee)
At bedtime - *neru mae ni* (nay-rue my nee)
Before meals - *shoku zen ni* (show-kuu zen nee)
Every four hours - *yoji kan goto ni* (yoe-jee kahn go-toe nee)
Four times a day - *ichi nichi ni yon kai* (ee-chee nee-chee nee yoan-kie)
Morning and night - *asa - ban* (ah-sah - bahn)
Three times a day - *ichi nichi ni san kai* (ee-chee nee-chee nee sahn kie)

CLINIC AND HOSPITAL SIGNS

Dermatology - *hifu ka* (he-fuu kah)
Ear, Nose and Throat Department - *ji bi inko ka* (jee-bee een-koe kah)
Internal Medicine - *nai ka* (nie kah)
Obstetrics and Gynecology - *san fujin ka* (sahn fuujeen kah)
Ophthalmology - *gan ka* (gahn kah)
Orthopedics - *seikeige ka* (say-ee-kay-ee-gay kah)
Pediatrics - *shoni ka* (show-nee kah)
Surgery - *ge ka* (gay kah)
Urology - *hinyoki ka* (heen-yoe-kee kah)

PART 12

EMERGENCY SITUATIONS

Key Words & Useful Sentences

Accident - *jiko* (jee-koe)

Has there been an accident?
Jiko ga arimashita ka?
aee-koe gah ah-ree-mah-sshtah kah?)

Automobile accident - *jidosha jiko* (jee-doe-shah jee-koe)

Have you had an automobile accident?
Jidosha jiko ni aimashita ka?
aee-doe-shah jee-koe nee aye-mah-sshtah kah?)

Be calm! Help is on the way!
Ochitsuke! Tetsudai wa sugu kimasu!
(Oh-chee-t'sue-kay! Tate-sue-die wah sue-guu kee-mahss!)

Ambulance - *kyukyusha* (que-que-shah)

I have already called an ambulance
Kyukyusha wo mo yobimashita
(Que-que-shah oh moe yoe-bee-mah-sshtah)

To be safe, I'll call an ambulance
Anzen no tame ni, kyukyusha wo yobimasu
(Ahn-zen no tah-may nee, que-que-shah oh yoe-bee-mahss)

Emergency Phone Number 911 - *kyu ichi ichi* (que ee-chee ee-chee)

I will dial 911 for you
Kyu ichi ichi ni kakete agemasu
(Que ee-chee ee-chee nee kah-kay-tay ah-gay-mahss)

Injury - *kega* (kay-gah)

Is anyone injured?
Dare ka kega wo shimashita ka?
(Dah-ray kah kay-gah oh she-mah-sshtah kah?)

Interpreter - *tsuyaku no hito* (t'sue-yah-kuu no ssh-toe)

Do you have an interpreter?
Tsuyaku no hito ga imasu ka?
(T'sue-yah-kuu no ssh-toe gah ee-mahss kah?)

Police department - *keisatsu* (kay-ee-saht-sue)
Police officer - *keikan* (kay-ee-kahn)

Shall I call the police?
Keikan wo yobimasho ka?
(Kay-ee-kahn oh yoe-bee-mah-show kah?)

Thief, thieves - *dorobo* (doe-roe-boe)

Please beware of thieves
Dorobo ni chui shite kudasai
(Doe-roe-boe nee chuu-e ssh-tay kuu-dah-sie)

It is better not to leave valuables in your room
Heya ni koka-na mono wo okanai ho ga ii desu
(Hay-yah nee koe-kah-nah moe-no oh oh-kah-nie hoe gah ee
dess)

Rob/steal - *nusumimasu* (nuu-sue-me-mahss)

What was stolen?
Nani wo nusumaremashita ka?
(Nah-nee oh nuu-sue-mah-ray-mah-sshtah kah?)

Someone stole this lady's purse
Dare ka kono fujin no saifu wo nusumimashita
(Dah-ray kah koe-no fuu-jeen no sie-fuu oh nuu-sue-me-mah-
sshtah)

Please make a list of everything that was stolen
Nusunda mono no risuto wo tsukutte kudasai
(Nuu-soon-dah moe-no no rees-to oh t'sue-koot-tay kuu-dah-
sie)

Tow truck - *rekka* (reck-kah)

I will call a tow truck
Rekka wo yobimasu
(Reck-kah oh yoe-bee-mahss)

Witness - *shonin* (show-neen)

Were there any witnesses?
Shonin imashita ka?
(Show-neen ee-mah-sshtah kah?)

EMERGENCY SITUATIONS

Dangerous - *abunai* (ah-buu-nie); *kiken na* (kee-kane nah)
Dehydration - *dassui* (dahs-sue-ee)
Desert - *sabaku* (sah-bah-kuu)
Desert area - *sabaku no chiho* (sah-bah-kuu no chee-hoe)

Deserts can be very dangerous

Sabaku wa taihen abunai desu
(Sah-bah-kuu wah tie-hane ah-buu-nie dess)

Temperatures sometimes go over 45 degrees C.
Ondo wa tokidoki yonjugo do ijo ni narimasu
(Own-doe wah toe-kee-doe-kee yoanjuu-go doe ee-joe nee nah-ree-mahss)

On those occasions dehydration occurs quickly
Sono toki ni wa dassui jotai ni hayaku narimasu
(So-no toe-kee nee wah dahs-sue-ee joe-tie nee hah-yah-kuu nah-ree-mahss)

The biggest danger in the desert is dehydration
Sabaku no ichiban okii na kiken wa dassui desu
(Sah-bah-kuu no ee-chee-bahn oh-kee nah kee-kane wah dahs-sue-ee dess)

When going into a desert, always take plenty of water
Sabaku ni hairu toki itsumo betsu no omizu oh motte itte kudasai
(Sah-bah-kuu nee hi-rue toe-kee eet-sue-moe bate-sue no oh-mee-zoo oh mote-tay
eet-tay kuu-dah-sie)

Rattlesnakes - *gara-gara hebi* (gah-rah-gah-rah hay-bee)

Rattlesnakes are common in desert areas of the American Southwest
Amerika no minami-nishi sabaku chiho ni takusan garagara hebi ga imasu
(Ah-may-ree-kah no me-nah-me-nee-she sah-bah-kuu chee-hoe nee tahk-sahn
gah-rah-gah-rah hay-bee gah ee-mahss)

Rattlesnakes can be dangerous
Garagara hebi wa abunai desu
(Gah-rah-gah-rah hay-bee wah ah-buu-nie dess)

If you see a rattlesnake, it is better to avoid it
Garagara hebi wo mittara sakeru ho ga ii desu
(Gah-rah-gah-rah hay-bee oh meet-tah-rah sah-kay-rue hoe gah
ee dess)

DUST STORMS

Dust storm - *hokori kaze* (hoe-koe-ree kah-zay); *hokori no arashi* (hoe-koe-ree no ah-rah-she)

We sometimes have dust storms in this area
Kono chiiki ni hokori no arashi ga tokidoki arimasu
(Koe-no chee-ee-kee nee hoe-koe-ree no ah-rah-she gah toe-kee-doe-kee ah-ree-mahss)

It is especially dangerous to drive during a dust storm
Hokori no arashi no toki kuruma wo uten suru no wa toku ni abunai desu
(Hoe-koe-ree no ah-rah-she no toe-kee kuu-rue-mah oh uun-tane sue-rue no wah
toe-kuu nee ah-buu-nie dess)

EARTH QUAKES

Earthquake - *jishin* (jee-sheen)
Earthquake center - *shingen chi* (sheen-gane chee)
Earthquake shock - *jishin no shindo* (jee-sheen no sheen-doe)

Earthquakes are not common in America
Amerika ni wa jishin ga amari okoranai desu
(Ah-may-ree-kah nee wah jee-sheen gah ah-mah-ree oh-koe-rah-nai dess)

FIRES

Fire - *kaji* (kah-jee)
Fireman - *shobofu* (show-boe-fuu)
Fire station - *shobo sho* (show-boe show)

If there is a fire, call the front desk
Kaji ga areba furonto ni yonde kudasai
(Kah-jee gah ah-ray-bah fuu-ron-toe nee yoan-day kuu-dah-sie)

FLASH FLOODS

Flood - *omizu* (oh-me-zoo); *kozui* (koe-zoo-ee)
Flash flood - *furasshu furado* (fuu-rah-sshuu fuu-rah-doe);
shunkan ni shinsui shimasu (shune-kahn nee sheen-sue-ee she-

mahss)

When it rains in desert areas, there are often flash floods
Sabaku no chiiki ni ame wa furu to furasshu furado ga yoku arimasu
(Sah-bah-kuu no chee-ee-kee nee ah-may wah fuu-rue toe fuu-
rah-sshuu fuu-rah-doe gah
yoe-kuu ah-ree-mahss)

This kind of flood is extremely dangerous
Koyu omizu wa taihen abunai desu
(Koe-yuu oh-mee-zoo wah tie-hane ah-buu-nie dess)

The most dangerous areas are gullies and dry creek beds
Ichiban abunai tokoro wa mizo to kawaite iru ogawa doko desu
(Ee-chee-bahn ah-buu-nie toe-koe-roe wah me-zoh to kah-wie-
tay ee-rue
oh-gah-wah doe-koe dess)

Never try to cross a flooded area
Shinsui saseta tokoro wo zettai wataru na
(Sheen-sue-ee sah-say-tah toe-koe-roe oh zet-tie wah-tah-rue
nah)

Life preserver - *kyumei bukuro* (que-may-ee buu-kuu-roe)
Life raft - *ikada* (ee-kah-dah)

HURRICANES AND TYPHOONS

Hurricane - *bofu* (boe-fuu); *huriken* (huu-ree-kane)
Typhoon - *taifu* (tie-fuu)*

*Japanese for typhoon means "great wind." Hurricanes and
typhoons are the same thing: massive whirlwinds spawned at
sea that sometimes strike land. They were originally called
hurricanes east of the International Date Line (in the U.S.) and
typhoons west of the date line (in Japan). Now they are
commonly referred to as typhoons by everyone.

A typhoon is coming tomorrow
Taifu ga ashita kimasu
(Tie-fuu gah ah-ssh-tah kee-mahss)

All outside activities have been cancelled

Soto no okonai wa zembu kyanseru shimashita
(So-toe no oh-koe-nie wah zem-buu k'yahn-say-rue she-mah-sshtah)

INSURANCE

Accident insurance - *shogai hoken* (show-guy hoe-kane)

Do you have automobile accident insurance?
Jidosha no shogai hoken wo tsukete arimasu ka?
(Jee-doe-shah no show-guy hoe-kane oh t'sue-kay-tay ah-ree-mahss?)

Burglary insurance - *tonan hoken* (toe-nahn hoe-kane)
Fire insurance - *kasai hoken* (kah-sie hoe-kane)
Health insurance - *kenko hoken* (kane-koe hoe-kane)

Do you have health insurance?
Kenko hoken ni haitte imasu ka?
(Kane-koe hoe-kane nee hite-tay ee-mahss kah?)

Is your insurance valid overseas?
Anata no hoken wa gaikoku ni yuko-na desu ka?
(Ah-nah-tah no hoe-kane wah guy-koe-kuu nee yuu-koe-nah dess kah?)

Life insurance - *seimei hoken* (say-ee-may-ee hoe-kane)
Insurance agent - *hoken dairiten* (hoe-kane die-ree-tane)
Insurance policy - *hoken shoken* (hoe-kane show-kane)
Insure - *hoken wo tsukemasu* (hoe-kane oh t'sue-kay-mahss)

PART 13

MEASUREMENTS

Japan uses the metric measuring system for all but a few traditional things like floor space and the size of lots and fields—and even then, if someone uses the metric system, they understand the dimensions involved.

With the exceptions noted above, to communicate any measurement concept to the Japanese it must be expressed in metric terms, as indicated below.

Room areas are generally measured in terms of three-by-six-foot mats called *jo* (joe) in Japanese. A six-mat room, for example (*roku jo*), measures approxmately 108 square feet or about ten by eleven feet. Land lots are usually measured in *tsubo* (t'sue-bow), which equals two mats, or approximately 36 square feet.

MILES AND KILOMETERS

1 mile= 1.609 kilometers To roughly convert miles to kilometers, multiply miles x 1.6 1 kilometer = 0.62 miles
10 miles = 16 kilometers
20 miles = 32 kilometers
30 miles = 48 milometers
50 miles = 80 kilometers
60 miles = 97 kilometers
70 miles = 113 kilometers
80 miles = 129 kilometers
90 miles = 145 kilometers
100 miles = 162 kilometers

10 kilometers = 6 miles
20 kilometers = 12 miles
30 kilometers = 19 miles
40 kilometers = 25 miles
50 kilometers = 31 miles
60 kilometers = 37 miles
70 kilometers = 44 miles
80 kilometers = 50 miles
90 kilometers = 56 miles
100 kilometers = 62 miles
110 kilometers = 68 miles
120 kilometers = 75 miles
130 kilometers = 81 miles

LINEAR MEASUREMENTS

1 inch = 25.40 millimeters or 2.540 centimeters
1 foot = 30.48 centimeters
1 yard = 0.9144 meters
1 millimeter = 0.0397 inches
1 centimeter= 0.3937 inches
1 meter= 3.281 feet
1 kilometer = 0.6214 miles

SQUARE MEASUREMENTS

1 square foot = 0.09 square meters
1 square mile = 2.59 square kilometers
1 square kilometer = 0.38 square miles
1 acre = 0.40 hectares
1 hectare = 2.47 acres

WEIGHTS

1 ounce = 28.35 grams
1 pound = 453.6 grams
2 pounds = 0.90 kilograms
3 pounds = 1.35 kilograms
4 pounds = 1.80 kilograms
5 pounds = 2.25 kilograms

1 gram = 0.03527 ounces
1 kilogram = 2.205 pounds
2 kilograms = 4.405 pounds
3 kilograms = 6.614 pounds
4 kilograms = 8.818 pounds
5 kilograms = 11.023 pounds

LIQUID MEASUREMENTS

1 pint = 0.4732 liters
1 quart = 0.9463 liters
1 U.S. gallon = 3.785 liters I
1 U.S. gallon = 0.8327 imperial gallons
1 imperial gallon = 1.201 U.S. gallons

APPAREL SIZES

WOMEN'S WEAR

Dresses and Suits

American	10	12	14	16	18	20
Japanese	9	11	13	15	17	19
British	32	34	36	38	40	42

Shoes

American	6	7	8	9	10
Japanese	22	22.5	24	24.5	25
British	4.5	5	6.5	7	8.5

Stockings

American/British	8	8.5	9.5	9.5	10
Japanese	20	21	22	23	24

MEN'S WEAR

Shirts

American/British	15	16	17	18
Japanese	38	41	43	45

Shoes

American/British	5	6	7	8	8.5	9	9.5	10	11
Japanese	23	24	25	26	26.5	27	27.5	28	29

Suits and Overcoats

American/British	36	38	40	42	44	46	
Japanese	90	95	100		105	110	115

TEMPERATURES

Centigrade - *sesshi-kandankei* (say-she kahn-dahn-kay-ee)
Fahrenheit - *kashi-kandankei* (kah-she-kahn-dahn-kay-ee)

To convert Fahrenheit degrees to Centigrade, subtract 32 from the Fahrenheit figure and divide the remainder by 1.8.

To convert Centigrade degrees to Fahrenheit, multiply the Centigrade figure by 1.8 and add 32.

32 degrees on the Fahrenheit scale (freezing) is 0 on the Centigrade scale.
  98.6 F = 36.9 C
  212 F = 100 C

Some other approximate comparisons:
50 degrees F = 10 degrees C
60 degrees F = 15 degrees C
70 degrees F = 21 degrees C
80 degrees F = 26 degrees C
90 degrees F = 32 degrees C
95 degrees F = 34 degrees C

CPSIA information can be obtained at www.ICGtesting.com
Printed in the USA
LVOW092157280312

275164LV00009B/138/A